Young People with Anti-Social Behaviours

The media today suggest that many young people are becoming involved in anti-social behaviour. But increasing amounts of legislation and ASBOs neither seem to have addressed the real issues nor solved the problem, and may simply add to the frustrations of all those involved.

Kathy Hampson's comprehensive guide is based on up-to-date, grass-roots experience of working with young people with anti-social behaviour. Including ready-to-use, photocopiable resources suitable for a wide variety of settings, it examines the background to these highly topical issues, enabling the reader to contextualise and better identify with the problems faced by the young people they work with. The easy-to-reproduce, tried-and-tested exercises:

- are for use with individuals or groups
- address the issues involved in offending behaviour
- can be easily modified to cater for a range of learning styles, abilities and maturity (and shows how you can identify which exercises suit which young people)
- include discussion scenarios, worksheets, cartoons, card games and creative activities
- can be used to dissuade young people from getting involved in anti-social behaviour, and to enable them to make better decisions.

The book includes an appraisal of current research on the issues surrounding anti-social behaviour and, in particular, risk factors that may be involved 'behind the scenes' in young people's lives. A section on working with parents helps them to support their children, improve their parenting skills and to know where, and how, to ask for help.

This is an essential resource offering constructive, *practical solutions* to anti-social behaviour in young people between the ages of 10 and 18. It will be invaluable for those working professionally or voluntarily in schools, with youth groups, youth offending teams, youth inclusion projects, faith groups, anti-social behaviour teams, or for anyone whose work offers the opportunity, or requires them, to challenge anti-social and offending behaviour.

Kathy Hampson is a Youth Justice Worker at the Leeds Youth Offending Service. She is author of *Setting Up and Running a Peer Listening Scheme* (Routledge).

nasen
Helping Everyone Achieve

Other titles published in association with National Association for Special Education Needs (nasen):

Living with Dyslexia, Second Edition: The Social and Emotional Consequences of Specific Learning Difficulties/Disabilities
Barbara Riddick
978-0-415-47758-1 (PB)

Dyspraxia 5-14: Identifying and Supporting Young People with Movement Difficulties
Christine Macintyre
978-0-415-54397-2 (HB)
978-0-415-54396-5 (PB)

Teaching Foundation Mathematics: A Guide for Teachers of Older Students with Learning Disabilities
Nadia Naggar-Smith
978-0-415-45164-2

Language for Learning: A Practical Guide for Supporting Pupils with Language and Communication Difficulties across the Curriculum
Sue Hayden
978-1-84312-468-9

Social Inclusion in Schools: Improving Outcomes, Raising Standards
Ben Whitney
978-1-84312-474-0

The Rob Long Omnibus Edition of Better Behaviour
Rob Long
978-1-84312-470-2

The Special School's Handbook
Michael Farrell
978-0-415-41685-6 (HB)
978-0-415-41686-3 (PB)

The SEN Handbook for Trainee Teachers, NQTs and Teaching Assistants
Wendy Spooner
978-1-84312-404-7

The New nasen A-Z of Reading Resources
Suzanne Baker and Lorraine Petersen
978-1-84312-441-2

Beating Bureaucracy in Special Educational Needs
Jean Gross
978-0-415-44114-8

P Levels in Mainstream Settings: Meeting the Needs of all Pupils
Lorraine Petersen and Ann Fergusson
978-0-415-43791-2

A Handbook for Inclusion Managers
Ann Sydney
978-0-415-49197-6 (HB)
978-0-415-49198-3 (PB)

Diversity and Personalised Learning
John Visser (Forthcoming)
978-0-415-46752-0

Young People with Anti-Social Behaviours

Practical resources for professionals

Kathy Hampson

LONDON AND NEW YORK

First edition published 2011
by Routledge
2 Park Square, Milton Park, Abingdon, Oxon, OX14 4RN

Simultaneously published in the USA and Canada
by Routledge
270 Madison Avenue, New York, NY 10016

Routledge is an imprint of the Taylor & Francis Group, an informa business

© 2011 Kathy Hampson

Typeset in Garamond Three by
Saxon Graphics Ltd, Derby
Printed and bound in Great Britain by
The MPG Books Group

British Library Cataloguing in Publication Data
A catalogue record for this book is available from the British Library

Library of Congress Cataloging-in-Publication Data
Hampson, Kathy Salter.
   Practical ways to work with young people with anti-social
behaviour : practical resources for professionals working with young
people / Kathy Hampson.
      p. cm.
      Includes bibliographical references.
   Juvenile delinquents--Services for--Great Britain. 2. Juvenile
delinquents--Counseling of--Great Britain. 3. Youth with social
disabilities--Great Britain. I. Title.
   HV9145.A5H3665 2010
   362.74'530941--dc22
                                          2009043906

ISBN13: 978-0-415-56570-7 (pbk)
ISBN13: 978-0-203-85265-1 (ebk)

Contents

Introduction

This book is intended for use by all professionals who work with young people displaying some sort of difficult behaviour. This would make it useful for schools, youth offending services, the youth service, anti-social behaviour units, youth inclusion projects, youth clubs, faith groups, uniformed organizations, social workers and other similar projects, of which there are many.

It is designed for use with 10- to 18-year olds of varying abilities and learning styles, and spans behaviour from nuisance to that which is actually criminal, looking to engender empathy and an ability to make better decisions.

The exercises cover a wide variety of topics, from criminal damage, theft, racism, bullying and truancy, to alcohol, drugs and more general anti-social behaviour. They are written in a mixture of styles so that young people who have a range of learning styles and levels of maturity will be able to access at least some of the material. This means that not all of the exercises will suit all of the young people – discretion is needed by workers as to what will work best with their young people. There is also a section with eight group work sessions covering similar issues. There are a number of games included that can be played either between a young person and his or her worker or by a group of young people. The last section is about parenting, which is a vital part of any behaviour modification work. The principles discussed will provide a basis for sound parenting work to back up other work being done with young people. These resources have been used with young people, some for a number of years, giving me an assurance that they are not only workable, but effective in encouraging change.

The book begins with some theoretical bases for the work, looking at the:

- *current law* in England and Wales, and what is in place for young people entering the criminal justice system;
- *risk and protection,* where a large amount of research into youth crime and anti-social behaviour has been targeted and from which much policy has been made;
- *learning styles,* which will give a brief overview of the current theories and how workers can judge what type of exercises suit which young people.

Part 1

theory

Youth justice

The system for youth justice in England and Wales (Scotland has a different system, which will be touched on later) has constantly evolved through a number of different pieces of legislation, the latest of which is the Criminal Justice and Immigration Act 2008.

Youth Offending Teams (YOTs) were set up through the Crime and Disorder Act 1998 with the purpose of preventing offending and re-offending by young people under the age of 18 (and over 10, which is now deemed as the age at which young people can be held criminally responsible for their actions), whilst also keeping in view the welfare of young people, as detailed in the various Children Acts since 1933. The Youth Justice Board oversees the work of the individual area-based YOTs. These teams are run differently in different areas, but always incorporate staff from five different backgrounds: the police, the health service, probation, social care, and education. This multi-agency approach is designed to meet all the needs and risk factors associated with their offending, as identified by practitioners.

Previously when young people were in trouble with the police, repeated cautions were used, but this caused doubts about whether this was effective. Now, when police want to charge young people with an offence, they can issue a Reprimand as a first response (except for very serious offences). The second time a young person is arrested and charged by the police, they can offer a Final Warning (again depending on the seriousness). If the Final Warning is not accepted by the young person, then the police may proceed to a prosecution.

The next offence is always taken to court, if there is enough evidence. For young people pleading guilty, the court only has two options: to give a Referral Order, or custody. Clearly this choice depends on the seriousness of the offence and a report, called a pre-sentence report, will be prepared by the YOT in order to assess this. If the young person pleads not guilty, then the matter will be taken to trial, which cannot then result in a Referral Order, but could incur a Youth Rehabilitation Order (YRO), discussed later. Young people can receive up to two Referral Orders, but a second is at the discretion of the court, which may want to impose a different order at this stage. Young people can also receive an extension of their Referral Order if they appear before the court again whilst one is already in place, but this can only happen once, and can only result in an order of a maximum of 12 months. When a young person receives a Referral Order, he or she appears before a Referral Order Panel consisting of volunteer community panel members. This panel decides what issues the young person should address during his or her order. The order can be returned to court after the halfway stage if the panel agrees to revocation for excellent progress.

When young people appear in court subsequently, the court can give them a YRO, which was brought in by the 2008 Act, replacing a number of other orders. The YRO requires young people to be risk assessed (according to their risk of re-offending, risk of causing serious harm, and risk of vulnerability) to decide what intensity of contact they should be given, and what elements should be included. These decisions are made by the court at the time of sentencing, and depend on a skilled pre-sentence report from the YOT, and also a comprehensive list of what programmes are available for use with each young person, as YOTs will vary as to what they can offer. The contact frequencies will depend on the intensity decided on at this stage (this also determines the contact frequencies of Referral Orders). Revocation of YROs can be applied for through the court at the halfway stage as a result of good progress, as long as there has been no further offending.

Young people who are sent to custody (receiving a Detention and Training Order – DTO) will normally be sent to a secure unit (or similar, such as a secure residential children's home) if they are under the age of 15. When they reach 15, or are convicted over the age of 15, they are likely to be sent to a Young Offenders Institution (YOI), which operates more like an adult prison. Young people of school age are required to attend education while they are there, and may also access other programmes devised to reduce their risk of re-offending, although in reality, if their sentence is short, they may not have an opportunity to do so. Sentences are from four months upwards, and usually consist of a custody element and a community element. The community element begins on release, and requires contact with a YOT according to their licence agreement. During the community element, they can be recalled to custody for breaching their licence agreement.

The Rehabilitation of Offenders Act 1974 allows for criminal records to be regarded as 'spent' after a certain period of time, depending on a variety of factors. This means that application forms requiring only unspent convictions to be declared do not need details of spent ones. Referral Orders are spent as soon as the order has been completed. However, if there was an accompanying order to pay compensation, the compensation order is not spent for two and a half years. YROs are not spent until a certain period after the end of the order, depending on its length. (It should be noted, however, that there are a number of jobs that require a full disclosure of all offences, spent and unspent, in which case all offences should be detailed. Enhanced Criminal Records Bureau (CRB) checks will also bring up spent convictions).

Anti-social Behaviour Orders (ASBOs) were introduced in England and Wales through the Crime and Disorder Act (1998) and became available for use in April 1999. ASBOs can be issued in four different ways:

1. in civil proceedings, which means the burden of proof is not as great as in criminal courts. Prosecution of ASBO breaches, however, is done in criminal courts;

2. in criminal courts on conviction of criminal offences, in addition to the main sentence (so called 'bolt-on' ASBOs);

3. as an interim ASBO, which can be imposed whilst evidence is being gathered for a full ASBO, but breach of which is still prosecuted in a criminal court.

4. County Court orders, which tend to be for adults.

ASBOs normally impose certain requirements, like exclusion zones where the person cannot enter, other people with whom they cannot associate, and activities in which they must not take part. They are for a minimum of two years, up to a maximum of seven years, but can be revoked in court should the subject be able to prove changes in his or her behaviour.

Other means available to deal with anti-social behaviour are:

- fixed penalty notices, which can be imposed on anyone over the age of 10, and tend to be for minor issues like littering and graffiti, and result in a fine;
- penalty notices for disorder, which tend to be for more serious behaviour, and can be imposed on anyone over the age of 16;
- Acceptable Behaviour Contracts (ABCs) which are written agreements between the perpetrator and the local authority not to engage in certain problem behaviours. These run for six months, but can be renewed if both parties agree. They are not legally binding, but can be cited in ASBO applications in court.

The youth justice system in Scotland is very different. Young people are not taken to court, but are referred to Children's Hearings, which were brought in through the Social Work (Scotland) Act 1968. This was to address the conflict between punishment for criminal acts and protection of children in need. It was felt that both these groups had common needs, which were not being addressed properly through the juvenile courts system. These Children's Hearings deal with all matters, both criminal and social care-related, for young people under the age of 16 (and in some cases 18), unless it is regarding specific serious offences such as murder. The age of criminal responsibility in Scotland is 8.

The system requires young people falling into these categories to be referred to the Reporter (referral paths can be wide and varied, even including the young person him or herself, but frequently the referrer is the police or social services). The Reporter then has the discretion to decide that no further action needs to be taken, that measures of support need to be put in place, or that compulsory supervision needs to be put in place, which requires them to refer to a Children's Hearing. The Hearing is made up of trained volunteer panel members who will then decide if compulsory measures are needed and, if so, what they will be. The Hearing has access to a detailed report on the young person. If compulsory measures are agreed, the panel will make a Supervision Requirement, which stays in place until that child reaches 18, and is also subject to yearly reviews. Earlier review dates can be requested, with the young person able to request one after three months.

For further information and updates, see these websites: www.yjb.gov.uk and www.cjscotland.org.uk.

Readers can contact the author using KHampsonBooks@aol.com

Risk and protection

Youth justice in the UK is linked very strongly to a theory of risk and protection, which has seen the identification by researchers of many risk factors for young people's entry into offending and subsequent persistence in it. There is also a set of identified protective factors that have been deemed influential in young people's resistance to criminal activity and desistence from it, once begun. These risk and protective factors form the basis of the assessment processes that are currently undertaken for all young people entering the criminal justice system (or the Children's Hearings system in Scotland).

The risk and protective factor theory is similar to that of the links between lung cancer and smoking. Smoking is a risk factor for smoking, but as many smokers will say, there are some people who chain smoke all their life and do not ever suffer from cancer. However, the risk factor of smoking is so strongly correlated with incidences of lung cancer that there must be some sort of causal link. Researchers have shown similar causal links between sociological risk factors and the likelihood of offending.

Researchers have looked into youth justice for many years (for example, beginning in 1953, West and Farrington conducted a longitudinal research project to identify risk factors for this with regular updates from their cohort every few years), and have identified a selection of factors that they feel are the most influential. These have been incorporated into the assessment tool used by practitioners, and identify 12 different areas of risk:

1. living arrangements

2. family and personal relationships

3. statutory education, training and employment (for those above statutory school age)

4. neighbourhood

5. lifestyle

6. substance use

7. physical health

8. emotional and mental health

9. perception of self and others

10. thinking and behaviour

11. attitudes to offending

12. motivation to change

These different areas cover a range of factors identified as significant for offending. Examples include those living in a deprived area with largely rental property, those with offending family or peers, those not attending any educational provision, those with substance use issues, those who indulge in risky behaviour, and those who have parents who have not sufficiently supervised them as younger children. There are some other significant factors that are taken into account at this stage called 'static factors', which include having a young age of first conviction, and having many previous offences. All of these factors increase a young person's risk of re-offending, which is the main issue youth justice services seek to address.

The exercises in this book are aimed at affecting some of these risk factors (for example, having offending friends increases the risk of offending), and building up the protective factors. This is also the reason for a section on parenting at the end of the book – the West and Farrington study showed poor parental supervision to be one of the most influential risk factors of them all. I would suggest that to tackle the young person without any reference to the parents is to reduce immediately the effectiveness of the work. This is not to blame parents, but to say that they have a massive role in changing their children and young people's behaviour.

This section is deliberately brief, but further reading on the subject can be found in the Bibliography.

Learning styles

There has been much written about learning styles and different types of intelligences, all affecting the way in which people learn. It is generally accepted now that teaching needs to touch a variety of different styles in order to be effective, with primary schools achieving this very successfully. Secondary schools have found this much more difficult, partly because of the constraints of exam syllabuses, and partly because they begin from an extremely academic view of learning as an activity.

Children and young people who have fallen foul of schools in some way will very often have begun well, but found that the strict style of lessons they were offered did not fit in with the way they learn, thereby effectively preventing them from achieving their best. It could be that those exhibiting behavioural problems in school are those whose learning styles are less often (if at all) incorporated into everyday lessons. This is sometimes demonstrated by the differences that teachers experience in teaching such young people, with some teachers claiming a young person is not teachable, and others seeming to imply that they have had minimal difficulty. Clearly there are other issues that could impact in these cases, but varying learning styles is a good starting point, in terms of making learning accessible. It is a matter of identifying which learning style an individual benefits from most, and incorporating that into his or her learning package. This presents a problem for teachers who need to communicate effectively with a whole class of learners each with their own style (and other possible barriers to their learning). This is where individual work can become especially effective, or group work that teams up similarly minded young people.

This book deliberately uses a wide range of styles, tasks and physical actions to enable the worker to connect best with each individual. Assessing learning preferences is the starting point (which will be discussed further) but, subsequently, workers need to continually assess how young people are responding to a certain style of exercise, changing if necessary, or just adapting its style of use. In many cases, merely using a wide range of activities will increase engagement, especially for those with attention deficit disorders.

Learning preferences can be divided into two separate ideological bases, either of which (or both) can be used: learning styles and multiple intelligences. There are many different definitions of learning styles, but possibly the most useful for this purpose is that devised by Fleming, who identified the VARK model (see www.vark-learn.com) of four different learning styles:

Visual learners – prefer to see things (pictures, visual aids and diagrams).
Auditory learners – prefer to listen (talks, discussions).
Reading/writing learners – prefer a more traditional school classroom.
Kinaesthetic – prefer to experience (like to touch, move, experiment).

Assessment tools for these styles are widely available on the internet and in books dedicated to learning styles. There are also other categorizations that could be used, like Honey and Mumford's (an adaptation of Kolb's original classifications):

- *activists* – prefer word showers, problem solving, group discussion, role-play, puzzles;
- *reflectors* – prefer paired discussions, observing activities, individual coaching, feedback, interviews;
- *theorists* – prefer stories, statistics, quotes, applying theories;
- *pragmatists* – prefer case studies, problem solving, discussion.

These are assessed by their Learning Styles Questionnaire, but an important aspect of their theory is that these styles are not fixed, but can be changed at will or by development.

Workers should use these theoretical bases as a starting point for their choice of exercises. For example, card sorting exercises easily lend themselves to kinaesthetic learners who physically move items from one place to another; auditory learners may prefer a discussion prompted by some of the scenarios or worksheet themes; reading/writing learners may prefer to complete worksheets; while visual learners might like to draw pictures, or respond to diagrams or pictures.

This can be added to the theory of multiple intelligences developed by Gardner. He felt that the question, 'Are they intelligent?' should be replaced by '*How* are they intelligent?' He has been criticized for using the term 'intelligence' when he should really use the term 'ability', but this perhaps limits the use of a talent to a particular area, when it could also be applied to other situations. For example, a professional football player who may not be viewed as being very intelligent in the traditional sense, shows great intelligence on the football pitch, which could be applied to other learning experiences, if he could experience them in a very physical way.

Gardner identified eight different intelligences:

1. *Bodily-kinaesthetic* – learn well by physical movement, especially involving movement around a room. They might respond well to role-play, drama, or games. They may show particular talents in certain areas like dance or

drama, and may be good at making or mending things, making them likely to enjoy constructing things or drawing.

2. *Verbal/linguistic* – learn well through the use of words, both written and spoken, and may respond well to talking, debating, reading, taking notes.

3. *Logical/mathematic* – learn well by processing problems, can reason logically, and perform complex calculations.

4. *Visual/spatial* – learn well through visualization, and can interpret information that is not described pictorially; tend to enjoy puzzles and conundrums. May also like drawing and craft activities.

5. *Interpersonal* – learn well through interaction with others, and enjoy debates, discussions and group activities; they tend to be extroverts, and can often show a good level of empathy.

6. *Intrapersonal* – learn well by thinking and reflecting on issues; may need to go away to think issues through before they can decide what they think. They will often be loners, who like their own company, and may not find group work helpful.

7. *Musical* – learn well if they incorporate music or rhythm into their learning; they are often musically gifted and can easily pick up new tunes. They will probably be able to remember lots of song lyrics, which might be a good way for them to memorize important information. They may respond well to auditory cues, making discussions or talks a good way for them to learn; they may relate more to kinaesthetic activities.

8. *Naturalist* (a later addition) – learn well when the experience is related to nature or outdoors; they may enjoy collections from nature or analysing related issues, but may struggle to engage with subject matter not related to their natural environments.

Using a combination from the two models of learning theory may provide a good indication of which activities in this book will suit which young people. Adaptations can be made to all the activities to make them more accessible to other learning styles, by substituting verbal discussion for written worksheets, for example, or constructing something out of physical materials rather than just using a picture, or acting out rather than reading a scenario.

Part 2

INDIVIDUAL RESOURCES

Introduction

The exercises in this section cover a wide variety of topics and use a number of different methods and styles. The main learning style of the exercise is indicated by a letter in brackets after the title: V (visual), A (auditory), R (reading/writing) and K (kinaesthetic). Some are a combination and most can be easily adapted to fit other styles, if the worker keeps in mind the preferred methodologies associated with the different styles (outlined in the theory section). Those with no indication are general enough to be used in such a wide variety of ways that the only limitation is the imagination of the worker!

There are two emotions resources at the beginning of this section, which can be printed out and used where emotions need to be identified and when young people's emotional vocabulary is small. One is a sheet of faces, giving a visual clue as to the meaning of the word, and one is a comprehensive list of emotions that can be printed out as they are, or transferred onto individual cards, as appropriate. These are more useful for young people without literacy issues.

I refer to response cards throughout this and some of the other sections (eg, 'true/false' card). These are designed to be printed off and laminated for use in a variety of different exercises, and are:

True for me/not true for me

True/false

Wouldn't do/would do

Good influence/bad influence

Emotions

Accepted	Appreciated	Affected
Afflicted	Aggressive	Aggrieved
Ambivalent	Amused	Angry
Annoyed	Antisocial	Anxious
Argumentative	Arrogant	Ashamed
Awestruck	Bashful	Baleful
Belligerent	Blamed	Boisterous
Bored	Brave	Calm
Caustic	Cool	Concerned
Condemned	Confused	Confident
Controlled	Controlling	Courageous
Cynical	Dejected	Delighted
Deranged	Despairing	Doleful
Disappointed	Disgruntled	Disgusted
Disturbed	Embarrassed	Enchanted
Enigmatic	Enthusiastic	Envious
Excited	Exhausted	Fanciful
Fearful	Frightened	Frustrated
Furious	Generous	Gentle
Glad	Gobsmacked	Grateful
Grumpy	Guilty	Happy
Hateful	Hopeful	Horrendous
Horrified	Hurt	Hurtful
Idiotic	Ignorant	Independent
Interested	Introverted	Jealous
Joyful	Judgemental	Judicious
Justified	Lippy	Loathing
Lonely	Loved	Loving
Mad	Maudlin	Mischievous
Miserable	Misunderstood	Monstrous
Mundane	Murderous	Nasty
Nauseous	Naughty	Negative
Neglected	Objectionable	Obnoxious
Obstructive	Offended	Offensive
Pensive	Persecuted	Perturbed
Pitiful	Pleased	Proud
Provocative	Quizzical	Raw
Regretful	Rejected	Relaxed
Sad	Sarcastic	Satisfied
Scared	Scornful	Sore
Seething	Sick	Stupid
Surprised	Tearful	Tentative
Terrific	Tremendous	Upset
Vengeful	Victimized	Villainous
Wistful	Worried	Wronged

Aggressive	Amazed	Angry	Annoyed	Cautious	Confused

Despairing	Desperate	Determined	Disappointed	Disgusted	Ecstatic

Embarrassed	Excited	Frustrated	Glad	Guilty	Happy

Hopeful	Indifferent	Indignant	Jealous	Joyful	Mischievous

Regretful	Relieved	Sad	Shocked	Surprised	Worried

Not true for me

True for me

False

True

Would do!

Wouldn't do!

Bad influence!

Good influence!

general anti-social behaviour

Including:

- attitudes to crime and anti-social behaviour
- rights and responsibilities
- time for change
- current assessment of activities
- reasons for offending
- scaling the problem

Antisocial behaviours (K/V)

The purpose of this exercise is for each young person to identify what behaviours they would be prepared to do (but not ones they necessarily have already done). They sort them onto the two laminated option cards, 'Would do' or 'Wouldn't do' (see page 00).

After they have done this, talk through the ones they wouldn't be prepared to do, asking why that is. Try to get them to identify who it would hurt, and what stops them from doing it.

Then take the ones that they would be prepared to do and write them on the Consequences worksheet (see page 00). Going through them one by one, identify the positive consequences *for them* – what do they get out of it? It might mean that they get excitement, money, respect with peers, etc. Make the point that no one does anything without motivation, so this is trying to unpack what the motivation for that behaviour might be for them.

After this, lead them to identify what the negative consequences might be (try to get them to identify who might be affected, how it might impact on them, their families etc). You could also ask them to identify emotions for those affected (use of the emotions sheet might be useful here).

Spit in the street

Drop litter

Drink alcohol in the street

Break windows in a disused building

Throw eggs at a house

Be cruel to a dog

Be cruel to a pigeon	Have a fight in the street	Graffiti on a bus shelter
Make a hoax 999 call	Fire a BB gun in a public place	Play loud music late at night
Throw stones at a car	Threaten someone	Verbally abuse the police
Kick a ball at someone's gate or house	Hang around on the street in a large group of young people	Carry a weapon

Get into a stolen car	Sniff glue or solvents in the street	Damage someone's personal property
Physically assault the police	Shout abuse at a stranger	Set fire to an abandoned car
Throw stuff in the street at people or things	Rob an adult in the street	Bully someone
Steal a kid's bike	Damage a parked car	Damage someone's garden

Truant from school 	Call someone a racist name 	Lie to the police 
Make a threatening phone call 	Stay out all night without letting anyone know 	Ride an off-road motor bike around the neighbourhood 
Break into a car and steal something 	Physically assault someone in your family 	Ask people for money in the street 
Throw a firework 	Start a fight 	Break a window in someone's house 

Steal a chocolate bar from a shop	Throw missiles at fire engines	Throw missiles at ambulances

Attitudes to crime (K)

This exercise allows a worker to explore with a young person what their attitudes are to different aspects of crime, and what some people say. Using the sheet with 'Strongly agree' to 'Strongly disagree' on it (which ideally the worker should laminate), ask the young person to take each card in turn and decide where they want to place it on the sheet. Keep control of the whole pack, so the young person doesn't just go through all the cards without discussion. After the young person has decided where the card should go, prompt discussion about their choice, maybe challenging them on why they think the way they do, and whether it is an acceptable opinion or not.

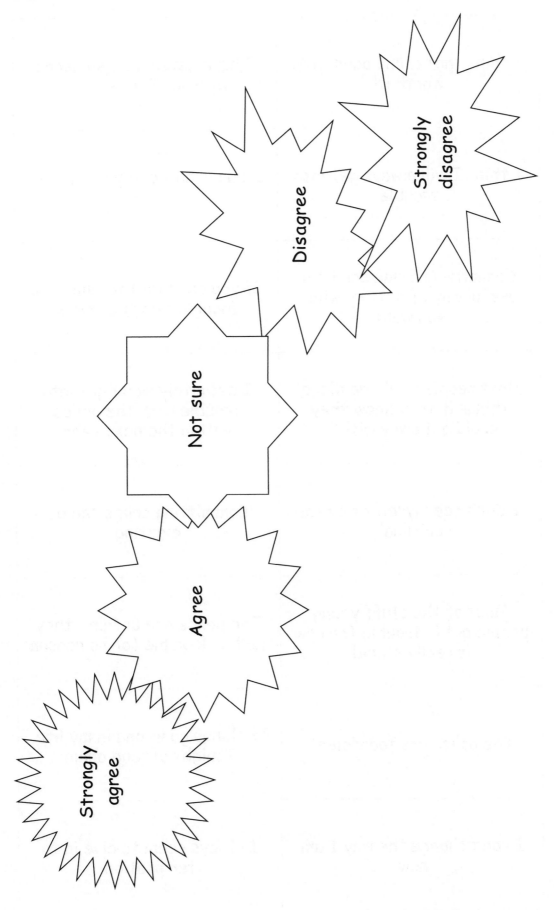

Strongly disagree

Disagree

Not sure

Agree

Strongly agree

I think that crime pays – it's worth it!	I have never hurt someone by what I have done
I think I will always get into trouble	Crime is now a way of life for me
Committing crime can be a useful way of getting what you want	If you can't do the time, you shouldn't do the crime!
Most people would do illegal things if they knew they could get away with it	I definitely won't get into trouble with the police within the next year
I don't see myself as a real criminal	Committing crime can be exciting
Most of the stuff young people get in trouble for now is really stupid	The police are unfair – they just pick on me for no reason
The police are too violent	If things go wrong in my life, I might offend again
I can't change the way I am now	I always seem to give in to temptation

Bill of Rights (R)

This exercise is designed to get young people to identify what they feel their rights are, and what they can expect out of the society in which they live.

Ask the young person what they think their rights are as young people in this country (and if they get struck by the thought that they have not got any rights, as they are always eroded by other people, systems and processes, ask them what they think their rights *should* be). Write (or ask them to write) their responses down on one side of the 'Bill of Rights' sheet.

Ideas to include in this could be free education, health care (including access to doctors and dentists), to walk around without being hurt by other people (which includes the right not to be bullied), to believe what they like, to work, to love and affection, to the protection of a police force, to complain if they feel that an injustice has been done, to take a matter to court if they believe they need to, to play in public parks, to walk on public footpaths.... The list could be very long, depending on their imagination, or experiences.

After the list of rights has been exhausted (prompt them if they dry up too soon), introduce the idea that for everyone in a society to have rights, then they must have responsibilities as well (for example, if someone has a right not to be killed when walking down the street, then people also have a responsibility not to kill, or that right will be violated).

Go through the list of rights that has been created, and try to come up with the corresponding responsibility for each (for example, if they have a right to education, then they have a responsibility to attend and to work; if they have a right not to be bullied, then they have the responsibility not to bully others).

If you know of certain issues that are more pertinent to that young person than others, you might want to develop the discussion when considering relevant rights and responsibilities (for example, if someone has committed a lot of criminal damage in an area, then the discussion about the right to a decent, clean community/street would be an important one).

Bill of Rights

How long? (V/R)

This exercise can be used in different ways, depending on what is required.

It can help a young person identify a point of change, or identify that if they don't change, the consequences could be undesirable. It can help motivate them to make an action plan for themselves for the next year, which may help them to access education or training more effectively.

If you want them to identify a point of change, ask them to write next to 'This week' what they are doing that could get them into trouble. Then ask them whether this will be the same next month, or whether there will be some of those actions they will have ceased doing. Develop this through six months and a year, each time challenging them to decide whether they will still be doing the same things or whether they will have changed. You can then go back to the start and put in all the positive things they currently do, after which they add, when they think it is possible, all the positive things they would like to be doing at the various points. They then need to be challenged about how they will go about putting this into practice (for example, if they say that in six months time they want to be playing football for a local team, help them to realize that there are smaller steps they will need to take in the meantime to achieve that. If they are able to see this (which would be especially true if they said that they wanted to have a job in a year's time, but are currently not accessing any training at all), then make a list from the exercise and action plan of what they need to do week by week, month by month to achieve their target.

If they are relentlessly negative about how they use their time, then go through the year plan putting in possible consequences of the actions that they will still be committing. Think about this in as wide a sense as possible, including the effects of being caught by police, the effects on their home life (and possibly whether they will still be able to be at home), effects on others around them, and possible injury that could occur as a result.

How long?

This week

Next month

Six months

One year

Risks (V/A)

The 'risks' exercise is a good way to encourage the young person to make a self-assessment of their current activities, and the risks they pose to them.

Ask them what activities they get up to during a typical week – good, bad or indifferent (if they say 'nothing', then start with sleep, which can move easily on to coming-in times, bedtimes, and when they get up). Give prompts to help them think of the types of activities they might do with friends (which may well elicit that they 'chill' – get them to be more specific!), family, on their own, at school, what they get in trouble for, what they have been arrested for, if relevant, what substances they use. Get them to decide in which column each action goes, but only write it in if it is reasonable (for example, I have known many young people who think using cannabis should go in 'doing ok', when it is illegal and could lead to their arrest!) Then get them to decide between -10 and +10 where they are on that scale according to how good their activities are overall. This can lead on to discussing what needs to change if they are not to be admonished or even arrested.

Risks (V/A)

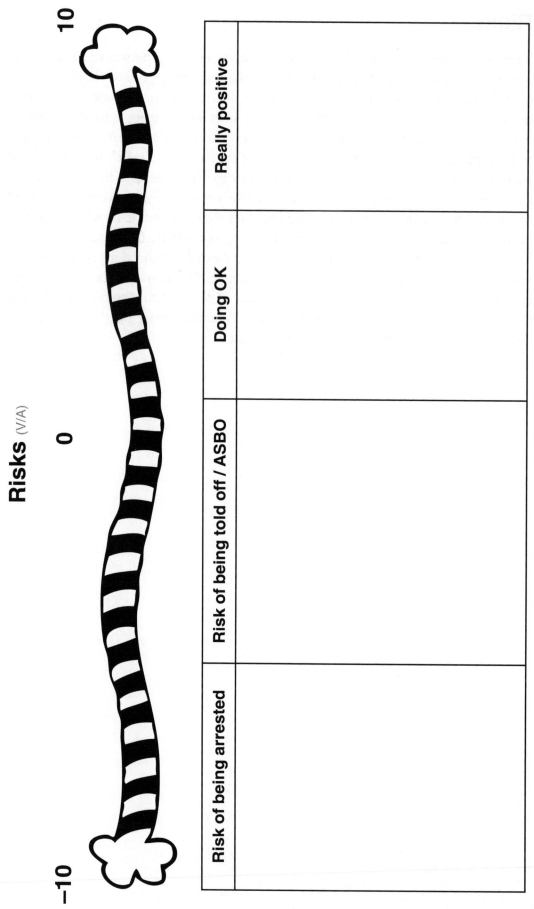

Risk of being arrested	Risk of being told off / ASBO	Doing OK	Really positive

Reasons for offending (K)

This exercise needs to be used with the 'True for me' 'Not true for me' cards (see page 00). Create a pack of cards from the following sheets, laminating them if possible.

Ask them to go though the cards, deciding whether each one has been a reason for a criminal or anti-social action in the past, or whether they have thought it.

After they have done this, collect all the ones that they have identified with, and try to group them together in themes (for example, put together all the ones relating to drug or alcohol use, all those that relate to getting angry with someone, and so on). There will be some rogue ones that don't fit into any categories. If there are one or two overwhelmingly popular groupings, these areas are going to be the ones to address in the future. Develop discussion about why these reasons are true for them, and what could be done to take away that reason, thereby reducing the risk of such behaviour in the future.

It was exciting	Why not?	My family do it, so it's what I'm used to
It's what you do	I don't care about the consequences	I was scared about what would happen if I didn't
I was high on drugs and didn't know what I was doing	I was high on solvents and didn't know what I was doing	I don't like obeying rules
I never get bought stuff like that	I enjoy breaking the law	I didn't stop to think
They wouldn't do what I said	I didn't know I was breaking the law	My mates were doing it
I wanted the stuff I took	I wanted money for drugs/glue	I wanted money to buy stuff
I wanted money for other reasons	I wanted to keep in with my mates	I wanted to look good in front of my mates
It was exciting	I was bored	I was drunk/ wasted

I wanted to get back at someone	It made me feel good	The chance came and I just took it

meone
me

nger

o help
e(s)

police

ust a
s going
gh

o prove
do it

ERRATA

Young People with Anti-Social Behaviours: Practical resources for professionals

By Kathy Hampson

The publishers would like to apologise for the missing in-text page references in this book:

Page number in book	Missing in-text page references
23	see page 20 *and* see page 90
37	see page 18
60	see page 19
67	see page 17
72	see page 19
89	see pages 23–27
92	see pages 16–17
95	see pages 93–94
101	see page 17
162	see page 17
164	pages 95–97 *and* see pages 23–27
169	from page 18
189	see page 17

Scaling (v)

Scaling can be a good way to ascertain how someone is feeling, or how they rate a situation at any given time. It can be repeated over time to build up a picture of change or progress.

Decide on a question to be asked, for example: on a scale of 1 to 10, how much would you like to change the way you are now, with 1 being not at all and 10 being completely?

The question can be asked to help young people identify how they can change a situation for the better: on a scale of 1 to 10, how good is your relationship with your mum, if 1 is awful (as bad as it could ever be), and 10 is perfect?

Then ask them why they have chosen that number – even if they have chosen a low number, as long as it is not 1, you can ask: why have you chosen such a high number? What makes it better than 1 (or whatever the number below is)?

If they have, for example, chosen 3, you could then ask: what would 4 look like? Get them to identify one thing that would make the situation better. Then look for when that is already happening and what the young person can do themselves to make it improve that much.

At a subsequent session, the same questions can be asked, with lots of encouragement given if they choose a number higher than the previous times.

This is a technique that is often used in solution-focused approaches, as it concentrates on how things can be improved, rather that concentrating on the problem.

Scaling

1	2	3	4	5	6	7	8	9	10

Including:

- hanging around in large groups of young people
- use of loud music
- using eggs against someone's house
- making hoax 999 calls

Just chillin'
(V/R)

It's Saturday again and you meet up with your mates. How many of you are there? Where do you hang out?

Draw a picture of everyone who is in the group you chill with (stick people will do!) Give some idea in the picture of where you are hanging out.

Consider the following people, and fill in the columns according to what you think:

Who are they?	How do they feel when they walk past your group?	Is your group any real threat to them?	Do they know this?	What are they likely to do?
Old lady with shopping bags				
Young mum with a pushchair				
Young person from a different area				
Two young children going to the shop				
A street vagrant				
Person of different ethnic background				

Put your headphones on!

(V/R)

Who lives in your street?
Draw a diagram of the houses and people in your street, as far as you know (you don't need to know names!)

What kind of music do you like?

Does everyone you know like the same type of music?

Write next to your street picture what type of music each person likes. If you don't know, put a question mark.

How many question marks do you have?

From this work out how many people in your street enjoy the same music as you!

Can you see from your picture how many small children or elderly people there are?

Why might these people have a particular problem with loud music (especially late at night)? Choose some feelings they might experience.

What might happen to you and your family if you carry on playing loud music?

What are you going to do?

YOU KNOW WHEN YOU'VE BEEN EGGED!

(V/R)

It's the summer holidays, and you are chilling with your mates. Someone produces a box of eggs from their bag and says: 'Well, what can we do with these?' They then look at you and say, 'I know, we can egg your house!' You know your mum would kill you if that happened, then you wouldn't be allowed out, so you have to stop them! 'No' you cry, 'You can't do my house!'

'Well, it's either that, or you do your neighbour's house!'

You know they mean it, as you have seen them egging people's houses before, but you've never done it (well, apart from that once on mischief night). This is different somehow, and you feel... (how do you feel?)

But what choice do you have?

(write or draw a behaviour choice in each box below)

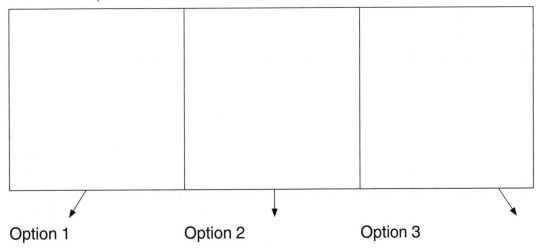

Option 1   Option 2   Option 3

Write down the consequences that you can think of for each option below the arrow.

 what do you do?

(V/A/R)

What Paul thinks about making hoax 999 calls:

Making phone calls to 999 is great! There's always someone to answer, and they will always talk to you. Sometimes it makes me feel important if I ring up to report something, even if it hasn't really happened. I don't want to hurt anyone, but it's just so exciting that sometimes I can't help myself. Sometimes I even stay around to hear the siren coming.

What Paul says if someone asks him:

It's a terrible thing to do. Just imagine what would happen if the fire engine went out to something that wasn't real and missed something that was! I would never do that. They have really important work to do, and don't need some kid causing problems.

Why do you think Paul thinks one thing, but says another?

Why do you think Paul can't help himself making those phone calls?

How do you think Paul would feel if he really did stop someone getting the help they needed from the emergency services?

criminal damage

Including:

- graffiti
- scratching cars

Just tag it!

(V/A)

You are waiting for some mates at a bus stop, and one of your other mates produces a black marker pen and starts to draw their tag on the bus shelter. He's a pretty good artist, but you reckon your tag is much more impressive. Also, you haven't had much chance to put your tag about and some mates have been suggesting that you daren't tag in a public place.

   He finishes his tag and hands the pen to you saying, 'Just tag it.' You think to yourself, 'What harm can it do', as you take the pen….

What do you think could be the problem with graffiti?

Write your suggestions on the wall:

Why do you tag?

WHAT WOULD STOP YOU?

Scccratch!

(V/A/R)

You're really bored! No one wants to come out and you are definitely at a loose end.

You sit on the park wall swinging your legs, when you see an old car parked up. It doesn't look like much cop. Not the sort of car you'd choose, that's for sure. What a loser! You start to toss bits of gravel at it to see if you can hit the car logo on the back. Actually you're a pretty good shot, so you challenge yourself to see how many bits you can get to land on the roof. One of the pieces of gravel obviously had a sharp edge because it made a really bad scratch down the side of the car as it fell off the roof. This gives you an idea, and you end up seeing whether you can put a dent in the door by throwing stones. The bigger ones obviously make the bigger dents, and by this time you're not that bothered that the car is looking even more of a wreck than when you found it. You think to yourself, 'They won't be that bothered. It was scratched already!'

After a while you get bored and wander off. Then you hear a scream and realize that the owner of the car has come back: she is a little old lady who has walked up with some shopping bags. You watch as she starts to cry at the state of her old, but previously well-cared for car.

What do you think the old lady feels at finding that her car has been damaged?

Why is she so upset?

How would you feel if that was your Grandma?

How would you feel if you had actually done that damage?

truancy

Bunking off!

(V/A)

You got to school ok, but that's where the trouble started! In maths, the teacher just wouldn't leave you alone. Going on and on he was. Couldn't he just shut up? All right… you couldn't do it! But surely that just goes to show what a bad teacher he is, right?

It's such a nice day outside that when you realize you have the worst lesson of the week next, you just think, forget that, I'm off!

But is it such a great idea in reality?

Think about what could happen, and write or draw the possibilities in the picture.

Try to think how each possibility would make you feel and select an emotion for each one.

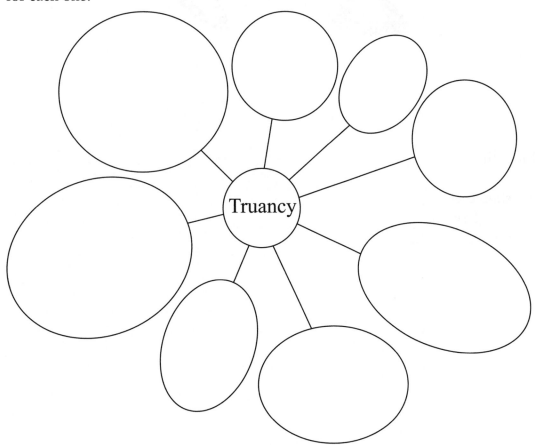

theft and burglary

Including:

- shop theft
- burglary
- attitudes to theft

BIG SHOPS, LITTLE SHOPS!

(V/A/R)

What do the big supermarkets think about people who steal from them?

What do they do about it?

You may not realize, but all supermarkets always prosecute people who shoplift from them. Why? Well... let's have a look!

Adam goes into a big local supermarket and walks out with a packet of biscuits. He's hungry, so why not? They certainly won't miss it!

Unfortunately the store detective saw what Adam did and chased him into the car park. He grabbed hold of him and took him back into the store in an arm lock. Adam by this time was yelling abuse at the store detective, hoping he would let him go. Adam didn't realize that the shop has a room set aside for keeping shop lifters while they wait for the police, which is exactly what happened.

What action has the shop taken to try to stop shop lifters?

This must have cost the shop a lot of money, so why do they bother when it's just a packet of biscuits? Try to make a list of everyone who suffers as a result of shop lifting in supermarkets (that includes you and me! Why?)

According to the Centre for Retail Research, in 2008 the costs of retail crime (including the costs of security) were £3,863 million, or £3,863,000,000! (http://www.retailresearch.org)

That's why they are so bothered, and that's why you are likely to get caught!

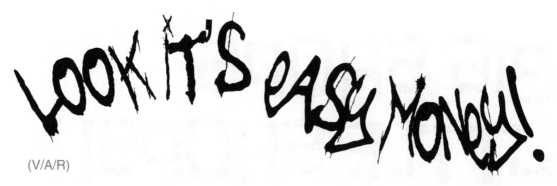

(V/A/R)

You hang out for the evening with two of your friends. They start discussing a house one of them saw earlier that had a window open even though the occupants were clearly out. They start to discuss the possibility of getting in, to 'just to see what's there'. After all, one of them reasons, if they are stupid enough to leave a window open, they can't be that bothered about their stuff. They turn to you and say, 'Look, it's easy money, are you coming'?

What could you do?

Option 1	Option 2	Option 3

What could the consequences be of agreeing just to go along?

Option 1.

Option 2.

Option 3.

Think of an emotion for how you would feel for each consequence.

WHAT WOULD YOU DO?

(V/A/R/K – act out)

You are with two friends walking back from school together. You nip into the local shop, as one of them wants to buy a top-up for their phone. While she is sorting this out, your other friend pockets a chocolate bar and gives you a wink. You all walk out of the shop together.

How do you feel?

Next day, you all walk to the shop again, and your friend says to you, 'I dare you to nick a bar of chocolate!'

How do you feel?

You all walk into the shop and your friend leads you round the back away from the cameras. 'Now!'

How do you feel?

Before you know what you are doing, you take a bar of chocolate and put it in your pocket. Then, walking smartly together, you go out of the store and on your way. No one has stopped you!

How do you feel?

The next day, your friend dares you to do it again, only this time you are to go into the shop on your own.

How do you feel?

You pick up the chocolate and put it in your pocket. You are about to go out of the door when the shopkeeper says, 'Hold it. What's in your pocket?'

How do you feel?

Guiltily you pull out the chocolate bar and hand it to the shopkeeper. Your friend sees what has happened from outside the shop and runs away.

How do you feel?

The shopkeeper asks you for your name and address, and calls the police. You can't run away because your face is too well known, as it's your local shop.

How do you feel?

The police arrive and handcuff you. They say something to you about your rights and put you in a police car.

How do you feel?

The police put you in a cell and leave you there.

How do you feel?

Some time later, your mum comes, and is really upset.

How do you feel?

The police put you in an interview room and question you about what happened. Your mum is there as well.

How do you feel?

You are charged with retail theft and bailed to appear in court.

How do you feel?

Was it worth it?

What would you do? (V/A/K)

You see a wallet on the ground which has obviously been dropped by its owner. It has full ID in and an address, but you decide to keep it instead of taking it back

You find a tenner on the ground and decide to pick it up before anyone sees you and keep it

A nice bike, of a type you have been wanting, is fastened to a railing with a bike lock. You decide to break the lock, as it's not very strong, and take the bike

A bike is leaning up against the wall, without a lock. You decide to take it, as there's no one around

You see an open window in a house, and decide to use it to get into the house. There is a nice phone on the table, which you decide to take

There is a garden shed, which you know has a nice bike in it, you decide to break the lock and take the bike

You see a Sat Nav in a car through the window, decide to break the window and nick it

Ask the young person to decide which of the theft-related actions they would be prepared to do. Ask them what the legality of each one is (each one is illegal, as 'theft by finding' applies when someone finds something somewhere and keeps it). To use this more effectively with kinaesthetic learners, act out the different actions, and get them to respond in the role-play, rather than talk about what they would do – they may not know if they just discuss it.

Develop a discussion about each one they would be prepared to do, possibly by asking them to identify why they would *not* do some of the actions. Ask them who would be the victims of each one, and how they would feel if someone did that to them.

Including:

- what your attitudes are to different people
- asylum seekers
- racist abuse
- stereotyping and assumptions

What do you think about people? (V/R)

If you like someone because they are this, tick the box. If you dislike someone because they are this, put a cross. If it doesn't make any difference to your attitude to that person, leave it blank.

Type of person	✓ ✗
Someone who uses cannabis	
Person who is white	
Person who is Asian	
A policeman	
Person who is HIV positive	
Ex-drug user	
Doctor	
BNP member	
Manchester United supporter	
Person who has bullied others	
Young offender	
A Chinese person	
A rich person	
Someone without any money	
A 'chav'	
Someone who likes rock music	
Recreational drug user	
Someone who smokes	
Someone who has a reputation for drinking a lot	
Someone who enjoys school	
A Muslim	
Someone with a flashy pimped-up car	
An immigrant from Africa	
An asylum seeker	
A magistrate	
A glamour photographer	
A television presenter	
A gay/lesbian person	
A professional footballer	
Someone who has been excluded from school	
Someone who has been in prison	
A Christian	
A solicitor	
A youth worker	
Someone who is a bit geeky	
Someone who truants from school	

Asylum seekers – myths and facts (K)

This is designed to challenge some commonly-held beliefs about asylum seekers. Print the statements on card, and cut into individual cards. Using the 'True' and 'False' cards (see pages 00 – 00), ask the young person to decide whether each statement is true or false.

Asylum seekers are illegal in the UK	Most asylum seekers are escaping war, conflict, or torture
Europe takes more asylum seekers than any other continent	Fish and chips were brought to Britain by Jews expelled from Portugal
Asylum seekers receive £39.34 per week	Once asylum seekers enter Britain they never want to go back to their country of origin
Asylum seekers are taking jobs that British people could do	Asylum seekers have been linked to criminal gangs
Asylum seekers are given a washing machine, TV, video/DVD player and a games console when they are housed	It costs each asylum seeker US$10-15,000 to escape their country
Britain receives less than 3.2% of the world's asylum seekers and refugees	Pakistan and Iran host one in every five refugees in the world
A refugee is an asylum seeker who has been given the right to stay	Asylum seekers represented just 7% of total entries to the UK in 2005
There are 9 million refugees and asylum seekers around the world	

Young People with Anti-Social Behaviours, Routledge © Kathy Hampson 2011

Answers to asylum seekers – myths and facts

Asylum seekers are illegal in the UK – false

Britain signed the 1951 Convention on Refugees so that anyone has a right to apply for asylum in Britain and remain until a final decision has been taken on their application.

Europe takes more asylum seekers than any other continent – false

Asia 37.5%
Africa 32.7%
Europe 22.4%
North America 6.1%
Oceania 0.8%
Latin America and the Caribbean 0.4%

Asylum seekers receive £39.34 per week – true

This is a third of what a British person on income support would receive.

Asylum seekers are taking jobs that British people could do – false

Asylum seekers are not allowed to work. Asylum seekers will sometimes take black market jobs like fruit picking, but such jobs are unregulated and are often seen as the work that the native population is unwilling do. They will also be very poorly paid, well below the minimum wage.

Asylum seekers are given a washing machine, TV, video/DVD player and a games console when they are housed – false

Asylum seekers are not given anything when they are housed.

Britain receives less than 3.2 per cent of the world's asylum seekers and refugees – true

A refugee is an asylum seeker who has been given the right to stay – true

There are 9 million refugees and asylum seekers around the world – true

Most asylum seekers are escaping war, conflict, or torture – true

Fish and chips were brought to Britain by Jews expelled from Portugal – true

Once asylum seekers enter Britain they never want to go back to their country of origin – false

Most do return to their country of origin when the trouble there stops. They usually have family they want to be re-united with. For example, most of the asylum seekers who came here from South Africa have now returned.

Asylum seekers have been linked to criminal gangs – false

There is no evidence to support this. Actually asylum seekers are less likely to commit crime as this would affect their application to stay. They are, however, more likely to be victims of crime.

It costs each asylum seeker US$10–15,000 to escape their country – true

It is very expensive for an asylum seeker to get to another country, often meaning that they give their life savings to agents who promise to help them.

Pakistan and Iran host one in every five refugees in the world – true

Asylum seekers represented just 7 per cent of total entries to the UK in 2005 – false

Actually, asylum seekers represented just 0.025 per cent of total entries to the UK in 2005.

NB: Workers should check these facts to ensure they remain correct, as some of the statistics may change; the weekly allowance certainly will change. All of these figures are available through internet research.

Stereotyping (V/A)

The object of this exercise is to allow the young person to decide what their first impressions of someone are, which can then be challenged through discussion.

Find some images of different people in magazines, covering a range of races, religious expressions (for example Muslim or Jewish dress), ages, genders, and clothing styles.

Give each person a name and go through each one asking the young person to decide what job they do, what their family is like, what their personality might be like, and what their attitude to them would be if they met them. Ask them how they would feel if each one moved in next door to them, and what they think the advantages and disadvantages of this would be.

Help to challenge some of the stereotypes that might come out of this by counter-argument and examples.

What did you call me?

(A/K – act out)

Phil and Sandeep are good friends. They get on well… most of the time! If they fall out, it tends to be about girls!

This time, it would seem that Phil has pushed things too far. After Sandeep got the girl on their night out (again!), Phil decided he'd had enough, especially since he'd seen her first!

He started an argument as soon as they left the place, and continued until Sandeep said, 'D'you know what? You just can't stand the fact that I'm better looking than you!' Although Sandeep said this with a smile, Phil was just not in the mood, so he gave a quick reply: 'Well I don't know what they see in a paki like you!'

And so ended a great friendship, all because of a bit of jealousy… or was it?

Do you think there was anything wrong with what Phil said back to Sandeep?

Why do you think that Sandeep was so upset by it that he now refuses to even talk to Phil?

What is it about racially abusive language that is so hurtful?

Would that language have been any more acceptable if they had always been enemies, and never friends?

Why do you think Phil brought Sandeep's different race into an argument that had nothing to do with race?

Does this show something about Phil's attitudes that is more deep-seated than just being jealous of his friend, if he is prepared to bring it into an argument?

Think of a time when you have said words about someone's race that have been hurtful… why did you choose those words and not something else?

What is it about your attitude towards different types of people that needs to change?

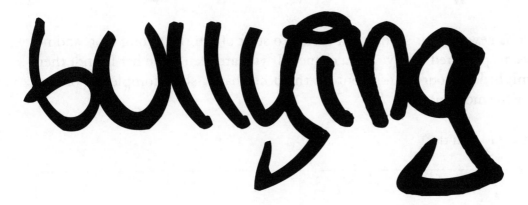

Including:

- school bullying
- 'I' statements
- being assertive

(A/V)

Sharon is new to your school, but seems to start off on the wrong foot, and no one seems prepared to give her a chance. If you are seen to be her friend, then you might lose your friends, but on the other hand, she's completely on her own at the moment.

What could you do?

Option 1:	Option 2:	Option 3:	Option 4:
How would you feel?	How would you feel?	How would you feel?	How would you feel?
How would she feel?	How would she feel?	How would she feel?	How would she feel?

Imagine you were new at school, and for some reason the other kids didn't want to get to know you.

How would you feel?

How would you cope with it?

What could someone else in the class do to make you feel better (try to list all the possibilities, no matter how mad they may seem!)

What would you do?

'I' statements (R/V)

Using 'I' statements can be a very useful way for young people to learn to communicate their feelings without being overwhelmed, which often ends up in abusive language. They are explained in the following sheet, which can be used both with young people who are being bullied to help them to express themselves more assertively, and with young people who bully others, to help them to control their actions more, which often come out of frustration and an inability to communicate effectively.

Go through the example on the page, and try to think of some more to show that you want them to identify how they are feeling first (the emotions card may be useful for this; see page 00), then the behaviour they do not like, and finally an alternative that would be better. When you are sure they understand the principle, apply it to their situation.

'I' statements

'I' statements are a way to communicate your feelings without blaming other people. You are more likely to be heard if you phrase what you feel in this way, because the other person is less likely to feel that you are getting at them!

I feel ....

when ....

I would like (or 'I would prefer it if') ....

For example:

Jim tells a racist or sexist joke.

Option 1: 'What an idiot, go get a life!'

Option 2: 'I feel offended when I hear racist jokes I don't want to hear anymore.'

Which response invites useful change?

Have a go!

I feel .... when

....

I would like ....

....

I feel .... when

....

I would prefer it if ....

....

What situations in your life would benefit from you using 'I statements'?

Young People with Anti-Social Behaviours, Routledge © Kathy Hampson 2011

Passive, aggressive, assertive (R)

This exercise is also useful for those on either side of a bullying situation. Those who are being bullied need to be able to express themselves assertively, so they don't inflame the situation, but avoid being passive, which can cause feelings to build up, often resulting in an aggressive action at some point. Those who are engaged in bullying may be doing so because they are unable to assert their feelings in another part of their life and have jumped from being passive in that situation to being aggressive in another, where they feel more in control. Helping both sides to be more assertive will reduce bullying, because the person bullying will not feel frustrated by other situations, causing a need to seek out control, and the person being bullied will not so easily be submissive.

Each section starts with a definition of the heading. Ask the young person to identify what they do that fits into any of the three headings. Try then to change a passive or aggressive response or action into an assertive one, so they have an alternative way of acting in their particular stress situations.

Assertive

Behaving as if everyone's feelings are equally important. Leads to no one's feelings being hurt!

Aggressive

Behaving as if your rights are more important than others'. This leads to other's feelings being hurt!

Passive

Behaving as if other people's rights are more important than your own. This leads to you being hurt!

alcohol and drugs

Including:

- facts about alcohol
- assessment of current alcohol consumption
- behaviours associated with drinking alcohol
- smoking cannabis

Alcohol – true or false? (K)

Print the following statements on card, and cut into individual cards, laminating for a more durable resource, if possible.

Using the 'True' and 'False' cards (see page 00), ask the young person to decide whether each statement is true or false.

Use the following answer sheet as an opportunity to discuss their answers, and increase their knowledge, particularly in the light of their own individual issues with alcohol.

The law says that children under the age of 8 should not be given alcoholic drinks	Alcohol is a drug
On average it takes one hour for your liver to get rid of one unit of alcohol	Alcohol helps you think more quickly
Drinking strong coffee helps you get rid of alcohol from your body	You can drink alcohol in pubs at 16 years old as long as an adult buys the drink for you
Drinking alcohol has no long-term effects on the body	Female drinkers who drink the same as men are more likely to suffer from liver or brain damage
Alcohol dehydrates the body	Alcohol is a stimulant
Regular drinkers can drink more alcohol than less experienced drinkers before they are over the limit for driving	There is one unit of alcohol in a small glass of wine or half a pint of regular beer
Alcohol can be addictive	Drinking alcohol is a major cause of road deaths

The answers: alcohol – true or false?

The law says that children under the age of 8 should not be given alcoholic drinks – false

In the UK, the law allows for children over the age of 5 to have alcoholic drinks at home.

Alcohol is a drug – true

On average it takes one hour for your liver to get rid of one unit of alcohol – true

But beware, because there may be more units of alcohol in a drink than you think! For example, one pint of ordinary strength beer contains on average two units of alcohol.

Alcohol helps you think more quickly – false

You may *feel* as if you are thinking more quickly, but your reaction times will be much impaired. If you try playing a reactions computer game with and without alcohol first, you will see a real difference!

Drinking strong coffee helps you get rid of alcohol from your body – false

Again, you may *feel* sobered up by drinking coffee, but this does not affect the amount of alcohol in your blood stream, which is still being processed at the same rate. Coffee just adds caffeine, which is a stimulant, to your system.

You can drink alcohol in pubs at 16 years old as long as an adult buys the drink for you – false

This is only true if you are also consuming a meal.

Drinking alcohol has no long-term effects on the body – false

Drinking alcohol above the recommended weekly amounts advised by the government may in time cause damage to your heart and liver. The current recommended weekly amounts are 14 units for women and 21 units for men.

Female drinkers who drink the same as men are more likely to suffer from liver or brain damage – true

Although this may sound unfair, the safe drinking limits for men and women are different (see above).

Alcohol dehydrates the body – true

Alcohol causes people to urinate proportionately more when drinking alcohol than when they are drinking water. This also causes a headache the following morning, and is why a good drink of water after drinking alcohol may help to prevent a hangover the next day.

Alcohol is a stimulant – false

Alcohol is actually a depressant, depressing certain parts of the brain. This explains why people often fall asleep if they have had too much to drink.

Regular drinkers can drink more alcohol than less experienced drinkers before they are over the limit for driving – false

Regular drinkers may *feel* less affected by consuming alcohol than occasional drinkers, but there will be the same amount in their blood stream being processed at the same rate. This means that a breathalyser test would not differentiate between the two.

There is one unit of alcohol in a small glass of wine or half a pint of regular beer – true

This also equates to a small pub measure of spirits. The problem is that people drinking at home tend to pour out more than a pub measure of any drink, and may not appreciate that different types of beers or wines have very differing strengths of alcohol. Always look at the bottle, which has to contain information about the units inside.

Alcohol can be addictive – true

People who consume a lot of alcohol can become physically dependent on it. There are more teenagers becoming physically addicted to alcohol now than ever before. It can be dangerous for someone used to consuming a lot to just stop drinking, which is why a detox through a drug and alcohol agency may be the only safe alternative.

Drinking alcohol is a major cause of road deaths – true

This is still the case, despite many advertising campaigns on television. People often feel that they are 'alright to drive' even if they clearly are not, because thinking is impaired after alcohol consumption.

Drink diary (V/R)

This diary can be used to diagnose the problem: identifying quantities drunk, of what, and the circumstances. This information can be drawn together to help construct an action plan for alcohol reduction, or changing dangerous drinking habits.

For example, it becomes clear if drinking only occurs at the weekend, but the amounts are so large that it becomes an alcohol binge every Saturday. There are guidelines on safe drinking habits, which are outlined in the alcohol group work session. These can be used to decide whether the young person concerned is at risk from their drinking or not. This exercise also promotes awareness of how much is being consumed during a night out, which can in itself be an inhibitor against drinking excessively.

The positive activities section can be used to encourage healthy pastimes, which can help if young people are drinking during the day when they could be engaged in other activities.

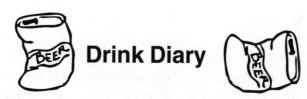

Drink Diary

Day	What/how much	Where/when/who with?	Positive activities (eg running, drawing, weights, etc)
Monday			
Tuesday			
Wednesday			
Thursday			
Friday			
Saturday			
Sunday			
Total			

With/without alcohol I would... (V/R)

This exercise can be used when young people are getting engaged in other anti-social behaviour only after alcohol consumption. This can be particularly true of young people who end up in fights after drinking, or who are more easily persuaded by their peers to get involved in undesirable activities after drinking.

Ask them to list the behaviours they tend to engage in when they have drunk alcohol under that heading. Then ask them to decide whether they would do that if they had not drunk alcohol. If the answer is no, then ask them what they might be doing instead. This often provides a way to identify alternatives to the anti-social behaviour, or may bring it home to the young person how much alcohol consumption affects their thinking and behaviour. This might be a precursor to using the drink diary.

With alcohol I would...

Without alcohol I would...

SMOKIN'!

(V/A/R/K)

You're round at one of your mates' houses. There's music, lots of laughs, lots of mates, and someone passes round a spliff.

You've never smoked a spliff before, and you're not exactly sure you want to now… however, what do you do when it gets round to you?

What are your options?

What do you know?!

Do a search on the internet to see if you can find five different health problems associated with smoking cannabis.

1.

2.

3.

4.

5.

But you're young right? None of that stuff's going to happen to you!

Maybe not yet, but although cannabis isn't physically addictive, it is extremely *psychologically* addictive. One you start you just can't stop!

consequences and the future

Including:

- consequences of actions
- how to get the future you desire

Consequences spider (V)

The spider is just a more interesting way of doing a spider diagram to look at the consequences of an action, and may be useful with young people with a lower chronological or learning age, or those with a visual learning style.

Identify what actions are relevant to the young person, then using a different spider for each action, identify eight consequences for each (one for each leg).

Consequences Spider

Crossroads (V/R)

Use this picture to look at the possible futures a young person might have, depending on how they spend their time.

Their position now is the start of the crossroads, but they can choose to either go down the negative route (the path with the devil), or the positive route (the path with the angel). Look at what the possible end-consequences are for them if they follow the negative route and write them at the top left hand side of the page (this could include prison, no job, no home, no money, criminal record, no friends), then do the same for the positive route (which could include good family relationships, good education, good job, money, girl/boyfriend, car).Then start at the middle crossroads position and identify what they would need to do from now to get to either side, writing the actions along the path. For example, the positive path might include attending school, getting exams, applying for jobs, not getting arrested, learning to drive, getting on well with mum, going to college. The negative side could include truanting school, being arrested, going to court, getting evicted, getting an ASBO, not doing school exams, staying at home instead of trying to get a job or college placement.

Ask them to identify where they want to go, and what they propose to do about it. This might lead to an action plan, or more work concerning the particular behaviours they want to stop, or need to stop in order to have a good future.

Crossroads

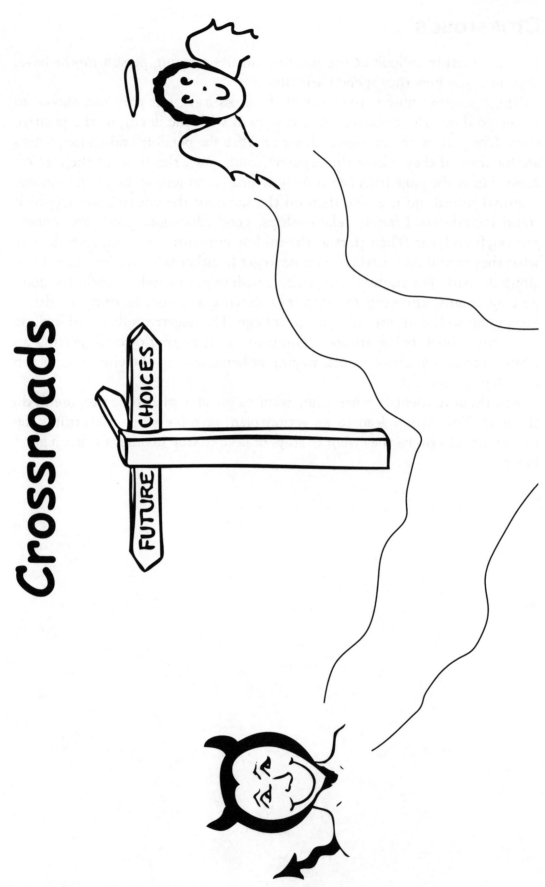

Personal goals maze (V/K)

This is another way of encouraging a young person to identify what steps they need to take to get their desired future, and may be more effective for some young people, depending on their personality and concentration levels.

The young person's current position is the space at the top left corner – they can draw a picture of themselves there – and they are aiming for the bottom right-hand corner. In that corner, ask them to identify what they would like to have in their future (it may be helpful to specify a time frame, such as five years' time). Then ask them to complete the maze from their current position to the future aim. Going along the route they have marked out along the maze, write (preferably roughly in the order in which they would have to do them) the actions they will have to do to get where they want to be. If they identify any actions that would not be helpful, or any they are currently doing, these can be written along one of the blind alleys, because they are not going to lead to their desired future.

Personal Goals Maze

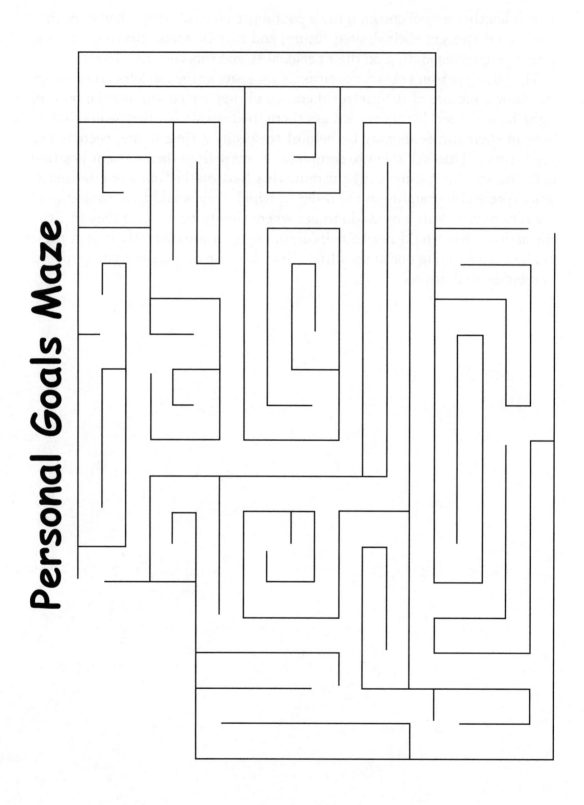

Possible futures

(K/V)

This is a practical activity to enable young people to see the consequences of their actions for their future – short, medium and long term. This exercise has several different stages and may take more than one session to complete.

Materials needed

Large piece of plain paper (A1 size if possible).
Small plain cards in a variety of colours (these can be bought commercially, or cut up from larger pieces to approximately 5 x 3 cm).
Glue stick.
Felt-tip pens.
Strips of paper-chain paper (ie strips of paper with gummed ends).
Two sheets of A4 paper.

Method

Ask the young person to put their name (or draw their 'tag') on one of the cards and stick it in the centre of the large sheet of paper.

Ask them to identify what they think might happen in their future (they will need prompts for this, and it might be an idea to get them to think from the closest in time to the farthest, for example, what they think might happen next week, next month, next year, next five years, etc). For each response (at this point try not to judge their choices, even if they seem fantastical) ask them to either write or draw it on a card with a felt-tip pen of their choice. Then they should stick these around their name according to how soon it might happen, so the futures that may happen next week need to be close, while futures that are years off need to be further away. Also, try to get them stuck in a logical progression, for example, if they say they want to leave school with GCSEs, and later they say they want to work as an electrician, they need to be in a line out from the centre, because one may depend on the other. However, don't be too prescriptive about this, as the method of achieving all the futures will be explored next. They can include things they would like to possess in the future (for example, a nice car or a house).

It is important to ensure that they think about both positive and negative futures (for example, they might think it is possible they could eventually end up in prison, so this should be one of the cards). You could position the negative futures in the bottom half and the positive ones in the top half.

The next stage is to explore how they will get to each of these stages (even if they are not practical). Using the strips of paper-chain, ask the young person to write (or you can write if they are not confident with this) what they have to do to achieve each future along the strip, which is then stuck in a loop between their name and the future in question. You may need to stick some strips together in order to reach, or link several futures together if they depend on each other (for example one strip to school attendance, and one from there to GCSEs, because one depends on the other).

The last stage is to transcribe onto an A4 sheet all the actions that need to be done to achieve the different futures (ones that are the same need only be written once). This should be done on two different sheets, separating desirable futures from undesirable ones, thereby leaving you with two sheets of actions – one leading to positive futures and one leading to negative futures.

Consequences (V/A/R/K)

Print the following 'Consequences' sheet. This can be used in conjunction with the Anti-social Behaviours exercise (see page 00), which uses cards of different anti-social behaviours and a classification according to whether the young person would be prepared to do each action or not.

For each action identified as possible for the young person concerned, write them down in the 'action' column. If there are various behaviours already identified as problematic with that young person, then those can be used instead, if desired.

The point of this exercise is to acknowledge that there are reasons why young people display these behaviours, otherwise they wouldn't do them. The positive consequence section is to identify from the young person what they get out of doing a certain action. They may say that they don't know, but will often be more forthcoming if it is pointed out to them that people very rarely do things for no reason whatsoever, so they are bound to have had some sort of a reason! Write all of these (which may be more about getting excitement than anything else) in the positive consequence section.

Next, identify for each action the possible negative consequences that could occur (incorporate legal action, feelings of victims, financial penalties, family disapproval and so on).

This opens the way for a discussion about whether the negative consequences outweigh the positive consequences for the young person. If they do, look at other ways in which the young person may legitimately meet the need that has been met by that action in the first place (look at the positive consequences to identify what these needs might be).

Action	Positive consequence	Negative consequence

empathy

Empathy (K/V)

Improving empathy is a good way to help young people see a reason for not behaving anti-socially. To do this, young people need to be able to identify and name their own emotions first. Only when they are capable of doing so will they be able to make meaningful sense of what someone else might be feeling.

To start this, use the emotions card, or the list of emotions (which could be made into cards if desired) – see page 00 – and use the following suggestions for developing self-awareness and an emotional vocabulary:

1. Ask the young person to choose three emotions from the selection that they feel right now.

2. Ask them to choose from the selection three emotions they like to feel and what might make them feel this way. Do the same for three emotions they do not like to feel.

3. Turn the emotions over, choose three at random and ask them to try to say what they mean, and then think of a time when they have felt those emotions.

4. Using the whole selection, ask them to sort them into positive and negative emotions.

5. Using the whole selection, ask them to sort the emotions into groups with other similar emotions.

6. Ask them to select three emotions and make a facial expression that might convey that emotion. This could also be done so the worker tries to guess what the emotion is.

7. Ask the young person to choose three emotion words they do not understand, and try to convey their meaning to them in a variety of ways (mime, what situations might evoke them, definitions). This could be done over a number of sessions, with different emotions being described each time, making sure the young person can still remember what the previous ones meant.

8. Ask the young person to choose three emotions they have felt over the past month or so, and describe the situations behind them.

How would you feel? (A/K)

Print the following cards and cut them out; laminate if possible.

For each situation, ask the young person how they would feel if this situation happened to them, using emotions cards or prompts where necessary (this may be a good way to encourage them to use a wider variety of more complex emotional words).

Your neighbour's dog is hit by a car	You see someone with special needs being shouted at
You see an old lady mugged	You watch a really sad film
A member of your family is hurt in a house fire	You see someone running from a shop having stolen something
You see a small child being bullied and having their sweets taken off them	You see police stopping someone on the street
Someone suddenly pulls a knife on you	The police stop you in the street
Someone calls your mum names to your face	You see someone running off down the street with an old lady's handbag
Your best friend nicks your phone	You see a couple kissing in the park

Young People with Anti-Social Behaviours, Routledge © Kathy Hampson 2011

One of your grandparents is ill and has to go to hospital	The sun is shining, and it's a really nice day
One of your grandparents dies	You see someone tormenting a dog
Your dog dies	You see a mother hit a toddler hard on the head in the park
You have a good day out with your mum	You see a Rottweiler running towards you
You get a really good report from school	One of your family members is diagnosed with cancer
You see a fight start in front of you between two groups of young people	One of your friends nicks some sweets from a shop when they are with you
You see a cat being hit by a passing car	Your mum starts shouting at you for something you didn't do
You go on the highest fastest ride in the theme park	It's your birthday!

Empathy scenarios (V/A/R/K)

These scenarios should be used in the same way as the 'How would you feel' cards (see page 00), except the young person needs to identify what the person or people in the scenario might feel. The first set of scenarios are brief; the second set have more detail.

Jason picks on a girl at school because she's fat	Chris was walking to school when he was jumped by someone who held a knife to his throat asking for money
Phil fails his exams so he can't go on to join the fire brigade like he planned	Gary was thumped for no reason outside his local pub by a drunk person who then passed out
Caroline thinks she's fat so she never wants to go out with her friends, even though she is of average weight	Nicola was offered some cocaine by one of her friends, who suggested that she was an idiot if she didn't try it
Christine thinks that her older sister gets more attention than she does from their mum because she is prettier	Paul went out and got drunk with his mates and they all ended up in a big fight, but one of them died as a result of being hit
Matt decides to take his brother's mobile phone because it is better than his, and he can get away with it	Sandy is offered cannabis by one of her friends, but she doesn't want to take it because her sister became mentally ill as a result of using it
David gets so bored in class at school that he always starts to mess around, always resulting in him being sent out	Greg's grandma was burgled while she was in the house, but then Greg finds out one of his friends did it
Jason got the sack from his job, because he lost his temper with his boss when he was told to clean up	Neil decides to carry a knife with him after his brother was killed in a street attack last year
Hayley did well enough in her exams to get the job she wanted	Darren gets into a stolen car that his friend has taken, but they crash into a lamp post. They are both ok but the car is a write-off

Anthony's granddad died last week from cancer. He had visited him every day in hospital for the past month	Leroy is living on his own and doesn't have a job or any benefits. He decides the only way he can get money for food is to rob people for it

A 13-year-old girl is constantly teased at school about her ginger hair. After some months of this, she decided she didn't want to go to school any more, and told her mum every day that she felt ill. Her mum stopped believing her after a while and made her go back, so she started to run away from home instead.	Jake and Pete walk into town, and are jumped by a whole gang of young people they don't know. Jake has his phone taken and Pete his wallet, which he had all his money in, as he was going to buy a birthday present for his girlfriend. They have cuts and bruises, but are not seriously hurt. Pete is developing an impressive black eye.
A boy is new to school, and finds it very hard to fit in, as he is from a different part of the country, and everyone says he sounds 'posh' because of his accent. He decides to try to fit in better by fighting anyone who calls him 'posh', which led to him being excluded from school.	Sarah was walking home from her friend's house, when a man she doesn't know stops her and asks her if she has the time. Sarah looks at her watch, but when she does this, the man grabs her wrist and starts to walk her off to a car nearby. He tells her if she screams he will kill her as he has a knife. Somehow she manages to twist out of his grip and run away. She manages to get onto a crowded street, which causes him to turn back.
A group of young people hang around a park together. They decide to go to the local shop, distract the shop keeper and steal some cans of coke. Shelley is part of this group, and has been told she must take some of the cans. She really doesn't want to do this, because she knows her mum will go mad with her, but doesn't think she has a choice.	Ben and his brother Andrew were playing football in a local park, when Ben suggested they break into the house on the corner, as the owner had just driven away in his car. Andrew wasn't sure about this, but went along with his brother. They had to break a window to get in, and then saw a woman come into the kitchen. She screamed and they ran off, while she picked up the phone to call the police.

Four boys, who are hanging around in a group together decide to steal a car belonging to one of their neighbours, because he has left the door unlocked. After a while the police start to chase them, and they end up crashing into a wall, killing one of them, and seriously injuring another. There are two survivors, who are remarkably unhurt.	Tim regularly hangs out with his friends drinking alcohol. They usually drink a crate of lager during the evening, but tonight one of them produced a couple of bottles of vodka. They drink it all, but after a while one of Tim's friends starts to look very ill and passes out on the floor, not responding to anyone.

Part 3

Games

The empathy game (K)

This game is designed to help young people exercise their empathy muscles, by requiring them to think about what someone else in a given situation would feel. Young people with a very limited emotional vocabulary can use the emotions cards (see page 00) to help, but those who have either already made progress or have a better ability to articulate emotions should try this game without them.

What you will need

A snakes and ladders board.
A die.
Playing pieces.
Snake cards (15), ladder cards (15), and scenario cards (60) printed out on different coloured card, so they can be identified face-down, cut into individual cards.
Emotions cards, if required.

Empathy has been described as being able to put yourself in someone else's shoes without getting stuck in them! I think that is a very helpful way to explain the word to young people. Make sure you define empathy before you start, as they may not know what it means.

The game is played like snakes and ladders, except that when a plain square is landed on the facilitator reads out a scenario card. The player has to identify what the person whose name is underlined would feel. If they answer to your satisfaction, they can roll again (but do not get another scenario). If they land on a ladder, then a ladder card is read out, which explains why they can go up it (and gives ideas of reasonable behaviour). If they land on a snake, however, a snake card is read out, which explains why they have to slither down (and gives ideas about what is not acceptable behaviour – which might cause some debate!) The scenario cards are in no particular order.

To avoid the young people choosing the same emotion each time, they can only name an emotion once (but they can choose one that someone else has previously chosen, because this still requires them to understand what it means).

This can be played with a young person and a worker, or a group of young people. Parents can also play it with their children. Some of the scenarios require them to think what the parent might feel!

Kinaesthetic learners might appreciate the use of a large floor board (which can be purchased from toy stores), in which they can be the playing pieces and they can throw a large inflatable die!

Scenario cards

Billy is 10 and has been knocked off his bike by an older boy, who then rides off on it, laughing	Sharon complained to her mum that she doesn't get as much pocket money as her friends	Sharon complained to her mum that she doesn't get as much pocket money as her friends
Amy finds out that her boyfriend kissed her best friend	Hilda has lived on the same street for 50 years, but hasn't been out now for two weeks because of the large group of young people gathering near her house every evening	Mr Smith owns the local shop, but doesn't know what to do about the number of chocolate bars he is losing when young people from the local school come in each afternoon
Mrs Jones knows her class are not going to do well in their exams because they are always messing about, but they won't listen to her	Mikey took some money out of his mum's purse for some sweets, and she has just challenged him about it	Mikey took some money out of his mum's purse for some sweets, and she has just challenged him about it
Andrew came in late last night, and also hadn't told his mum where he was	Dylan threw eggs at his neighbour's house because she told him off for playing with his ball in the street	Leroy picked some flowers for his mum, but they were from his neighbour's garden

Young People with Anti-Social Behaviours, Routledge © Kathy Hampson 2011

Leroy picked some flowers for his mum, but they were from his neighbour's garden	Anya was walking through town when another girl came up and took her mobile phone off her	James saw his younger brother being picked on by a bigger kid in school
James saw his younger brother being picked on by a bigger kid in school	James saw his younger brother being picked on by a bigger kid in school	David was challenged to a fight by another boy in his class who was known as being hard
Hardeep wanted to join her friends in the park but her dad wouldn't let her	Issam decided to take a knife to school because he had been picked on yesterday	Rachel was challenged to have a spliff by some of the others girls in her class. She'd never tried it before
Ishmael's dog cut its paw on a bottle that had been left smashed on the pavement	Sandra always had her music turned up loud, because she thought it sounded better like that, but her neighbour had a small baby that wouldn't sleep because of the noise	Sammy was a train driver who slammed on the brakes as a missile hit his windscreen from a group of kids playing by the tracks

Bobby used his air gun to pop at pigeons sitting on the fence, but missed and hit his neighbour's little girl in the face	Bobby used his air gun to pop at pigeons sitting on the fence, but missed and hit his neighbour's little girl in the face	Gavin's friends arrived at his house cruising in a car one of them had nicked from the next street. They tell Gavin to get in
Darren sees a group of lads driving off in his car, which he'd just parked outside his house	Amy heard a noise in the night and crept downstairs to see what it was. She disturbed some lads who'd broken in through her kitchen window	Amy heard a noise in the night and crept downstairs to see what it was. She disturbed some lads who'd broken in through her kitchen window
Bobby used his air gun to pop at pigeons sitting on the fence, but missed and hit his neighbour's little girl in the face	Helen was shocked to discover her 15-year-old son sniffing glue in his bedroom	Louise was waiting up for her daughter, who didn't get in from her night out until 3 am
Carol and her daughter Michelle were always arguing, but things reached a crisis when Michelle told her mum she was pregnant	Carol and her daughter Michelle were always arguing, but things reached a crisis when Michelle told her mum she was pregnant	Pete came home from school covered in bruises from the latest fight he'd had at school, and lost

Young People with Anti-Social Behaviours, Routledge © Kathy Hampson 2011

Pete came home from school covered in bruises from the latest fight he'd had at school, and lost. His mum grounded him	Sam was stopped by the police in the street, who were investigating some local burglaries. Sam lost his temper and started swearing at them	Sam was stopped by the police in the street, who were investigating some local burglaries. Sam lost his temper and started swearing at them
Ben rang 999 to report a fire, but this was a lie. The operator recognized his voice as someone who had made hoax calls before	Ben rang 999 to report a fire, but this was a lie. The operator recognized his voice as someone who had made hoax calls before	Charlie and his friends liked to throw stuff at passing fire engines to see if they could hit them. The fire fighters had to swerve more than once to avoid being hit
Tim always put his tag on a bus shelter if he was waiting there. When he did it to a neighbour's fence, she complained to his mum	Tim always put his tag on a bus shelter if he was waiting there. When he did it to a neighbour's fence, she complained to his mum	Chloe had decided she wasn't going to stay for her maths class, as she hated the teacher. School rang her mum to say she was missing
Chloe had decided she wasn't going to stay for her maths class, as she hated the teacher. School rang her mum to say she was missing	Tom and his friends were 16, but always tried to get shops to sell them alcohol. When a local shop keeper refused, they threatened to firebomb his shop	A group of lads started to light fires in wheelie bins in their street. One of the neighbours complained as his bin went up in smoke

Young People with Anti-Social Behaviours, Routledge © Kathy Hampson 2011

A group of lads started to light fires in wheelie bins in their street. One of the neighbours complained as his bin went up in smoke. Den didn't really want to join in, but daren't refuse	Elizabeth saw that her window boxes had been destroyed in the night. She had no garden to put plants in	Phil and his mates always rode their motorbikes on a bit of waste ground near their houses. Some of the neighbours complained about the noise. One of them reported them to the police
Phil and his mates always rode their motorbikes on a bit of waste ground near their houses. Some of the neighbours complained about the noise. One of them reported them to the police	Craig put a key scratch down his neighbour's car, after she'd complained at him for playing loud music all night	Nico threw a firework to his mate, who caught it and threw it back. The firework exploded in Nico's face, causing severe burns
Nico threw a firework to his mate, who caught it and threw it back. The firework exploded in Nico's face, causing severe burns	Steven shouted racist abuse at another lad, because he had designer gear	Steven shouted racist abuse at another lad, because he had designer gear
The lads' football landed in Florrie's garden yet again, breaking her prize roses	A lad walked past Fiona, who had her baby in a buggy. He spat down at the pavement, but some of it landed on the baby's coat	Alex was offered a bike for a tenner from his mate. He knew that his mate had been done before for stealing a bike, and refused

Snake Cards

You spat in the street	You dropped a crisp packet instead of putting it in the bin	You tagged a bus shelter with a marker pen
You pushed your little brother around until he shared his sweets with you	Your mum asked you to make her a cup of tea, but you refused, saying you were busy	Your mum asked you to tidy your room, but you refused and slammed out of the house
You pick some flowers from the park – no one will miss them…	You kick the cat as you walk past it, because you're not allowed out	You don't tell your mum when you're coming home, and then stay out all night
Your mum asked you to be home for 10, but you try to sneak in at midnight	You play football in the street and knock the wing mirror off your neighbour's car	You refuse to turn down your music, even though your mum keeps saying you will get her evicted
You hang out in a disused factory building with your mates, and break the windows for fun	You and your friends start a fire on the grass down the road to hang out by in the evening	You raid your mum's alcohol to take to your mate's tonight, as you want to get plastered

Ladder Cards

You make your mum a cup of tea because she looks tired	You volunteer to baby-sit for your little sister	You volunteer to help your elderly neighbour tidy up her garden
You wash your neighbour's car	You go to the shop for your mum, who wants some milk and bread	You get up without having to be shouted at by your mum
You actually complete all your homework	You pick up a little kid from the ground who's fallen off his bike	You stop one of your friends picking on the little boy down the road
You buy your mum flowers for her birthday	You volunteer to make the tea (and it's not a takeaway!)	You help clean up the litter in the local park
You don't accept the offer of a cheap mobile phone, because you know it will have been stolen	You take yourself outside to calm down instead of kicking off	You help take an elderly relative shopping

RIGHT OR WRONG PURSUIT (V/A/R/K)

This game is a mixture of many subjects, allowing young people to think about different aspects of their behaviour at the same time. This is useful when there are several issues to be addressed, and allows the worker also to assess the different areas within the game.

The areas covered are anger management, self-esteem, offending behaviour, drugs and alcohol, feelings and emotions, friendships, bullying, behaviour, and self-control. The game can be played with a group of young people, or with a young person and a worker.

What you will need

A game board of the type that consists of different coloured squares in a wheel shape, with places for the collection of wedges in different colours, and the accompanying wedges and their cases for playing pieces (there are several games like this on the market).
A die.
The following cards, printed on a different colour card for each category.
A categories card with the card colours added to the category types, also detailing which colour this relates to on the board, if different.

The game starts with all playing pieces in the middle. The person going first throws the die and moves their piece. They have to answer a question that relates to the colour on which they land. If they get this question right, they can throw again until they get a question wrong. If they enter the wedge square and if they give a correct answer to the question, they get a wedge of that colour. The object of the game is to collect a wedge of every different colour, and then get to the middle again, where they answer a question from a category chosen by the other players.

Card categories

Card colour   **Colour on board**

◯   Anger management   ◯

◯   Alcohol, drugs and all that   ◯

◯   Emotions   ◯

◯   Offending   ◯

◯   Self-esteem   ◯

◯   Pot luck!   ◯

Anger management

Name three different things you do when you are angry	How can anger change things at school or work?	Name two triggers that make you mad and say how you could avoid them
Name two things that change in your body when you get mad	Name two areas of your life that can be affected by your anger	Can you think of a time where you were angry but managed not to kick off? What did you do?
Is anger an emotion? Why?	Name one person who can help you when you are angry	How can anger affect your family and friends?
True or false: Breaking things when you are angry can get you in trouble with the police	True or false: If you drink alcohol when you are angry it will make the anger go away	True or false: Being assertive is a good way to deal with angry feelings

True or false: If I have a fight with someone my age the police can't charge me	True or false: If you keep your feelings inside you are more likely to blow	True or false: When you are angry, your eye sight is sharper
True or false: Violence is the best way to get what you want	True or false: Everyone gets mad when people shout at them	True or false: When you get angry, adrenaline is released in your body
True or false: Your heart beats faster when you get angry	True or false: When you get angry you breathe faster	True or false: You are likely to feel down after an angry outburst
True or false: I get angry if I am stopped by the police	On a scale of 0 to 10, how angry would you get if… You were blamed for doing something you didn't do	On a scale of 0 to 10, how angry would you get if… You were grassed up by someone

On a scale of 0 to 10, how angry would you get if… You were lied to by a friend	On a scale of 0 to 10, how angry would you get if… You were called names by someone	On a scale of 0 to 10, how angry would you get if… Your mum was slagged off by someone
On a scale of 0 to 10, how angry would you get if… You were made fun of by a friend	On a scale of 0 to 10, how angry would you get if… Someone gave you a dirty look	On a scale of 0 to 10, how angry would you get if… You were told to turn your music down by a neighbour
On a scale of 0 to 10, how angry would you get if… A friend told someone else one of your secrets	On a scale of 0 to 10, how angry would you get if… A shopkeeper refused to serve you	On a scale of 0 to 10, how angry would you get if… A neighbour complained about you
On a scale of 0 to 10, how angry would you get if… You were shouted at	On a scale of 0 to 10, how angry would you get if… People were talking about you behind your back	On a scale of 0 to 10, how angry would you get if… Someone threatened you

On a scale of 0 to 10, how angry would you get if… Someone pushed you	On a scale of 0 to 10, how angry would you get if… Someone you don't know shouts abuse at you in the street	On a scale of 0 to 10, how angry would you get if… You aren't allowed to do what you want
On a scale of 0 to 10, how angry would you get if… Something was unfair	On a scale of 0 to 10, how angry would you get if… You made a mistake	On a scale of 0 to 10, how angry would you get if… Someone made you feel stupid
On a scale of 0 to 10, how angry would you get if… You were searched by the police	On a scale of 0 to 10, how angry would you get if… Someone knocked into you by accident and made you spill your drink	On a scale of 0 to 10, how angry would you get if… A little kid was annoying you

Drugs, alcohol and all that

True or false: You can drink alcohol in pubs at 16 years old as long as an adult buys the drink for you	True or false: Alcohol helps you think more quickly	True or false: Drinking strong coffee helps you get rid of alcohol from your body
True or false: Drinking alcohol has no long-term effects on the body	True or false: Alcohol is a drug	True or false: On average it takes one hour for your liver to get rid of one unit of alcohol
True or false: Female drinkers who drink the same as men are more likely to suffer from liver or brain damage	True or false: Alcohol dehydrates the body	True or false: The law says that children under the age of 8 should not be given alcoholic drinks
True or false: Alcohol can be addictive	True or false: There is one unit of alcohol in a small glass of wine or half a pint of regular beer	True or false: Regular drinkers can drink more alcohol than less experienced drinkers before they are over the limit for driving
True or false: Eating before and between drinks helps reduce the effects of alcohol	True or false: Your size is an important factor in how much you can drink safely	True or false: Drinking alcohol is a major cause of road deaths

True or false: Heroin is a class A drug	True or false: Cannabis is a legal drug now	True or false: Poppers are illegal
True or false: Heroin is a stimulant	True or false: Magic mushrooms are a hallucinogen	True or false: You can get a life sentence in prison for dealing class A drugs
Name two other terms for cannabis	Name two other terms for heroin	Name two other terms for cocaine
Name two other terms for amphetamines	Name three class A drugs	True or false: Selling solvents to under-16s is illegal
True or false: It is illegal to buy cigarettes under the age of 16	True or false: You can die instantly from sniffing solvents	True or false: It is illegal to possess cannabis now

True or false: Alcohol is a factor in 40% of household fires	How many units of alcohol are in a pint of ordinary strength beer?	What do you think… Giving cannabis to a friend for free isn't illegal
What do you think… Selling prescribed drugs to someone else is illegal	What do you think… Buying alcohol for someone under 18 isn't a big deal	What do you think? Having illegal drugs at home for personal use isn't a big deal
What do you think… It's ok to spike someone's drink with more alcohol without them knowing	What do you think… Mixing drugs and alcohol is dangerous	What do you think… If your parents/carers are drug addicts, you will become one too
What do you think… Drug dealers care about their customers	What do you think… Smoking cannabis leads to the use of harder drugs	What do you think… Someone who drinks every day has an alcohol problem
What do you think… Trying drugs once could lead to becoming hooked	What do you think… Drug dealers cut and mix drugs to make more profit	What do you think… All drug addicts and alcoholics commit crimes

Emotions

What makes you feel… Surprised?	What makes you feel… Happy?	What makes you feel… Sad?
What makes you feel… Angry?	What makes you feel… Frustrated?	What makes you feel… Guilty?
What makes you feel… Shy?	What makes you feel… Miserable?	What makes you feel… Anxious?
What makes you feel… Confused?	What makes you feel… Peaceful?	What makes you feel… Hopeful?
What makes you feel… Loved?	What makes you feel… Disappointed?	What makes you feel… lonely?

What makes you feel... Frightened?	What makes you feel... Grumpy?	What makes you feel... Worried?
What makes you feel... Naughty?	What makes you feel... Relaxed?	What makes you feel... Stubborn?
What makes you feel... Shocked?	What makes you feel... Suspicious?	What makes you feel... Enthusiastic?
What makes you feel... Abandoned?	What makes you feel... Paranoid?	What makes you feel... Gloomy?
What makes you feel... Yucky?	What makes you feel... Aggressive?	What makes you feel... Generous?

What makes you feel... Ashamed?	What makes you feel... Innocent?	What makes you feel... Envious?
What makes you feel... Proud?	What makes you feel... Mischievous?	What makes you feel... Excited?
What makes you feel... Disgusted?	What makes you feel... Relieved?	What makes you feel... Amused?
What makes you feel... Embarrassed?	What makes you feel... Cautious?	What makes you feel... Sorry?
What makes you feel... Misunderstood?	What makes you feel... Bored?	What makes you feel... Negative?

Offending behaviour

What do you think… I don't see myself as a real criminal	What do you think… I definitely won't get into trouble with the police within the next year	What do you think… If you can't do the time, you shouldn't do the crime!
What do you think… Most people would do illegal things if they knew they could get away with it	What do you think… If things go wrong with me, I might get in trouble with the police	What do you think… I always seem to give in to temptation
What do you think… Many so-called crimes are not really wrong	What do you think… I believe in living for now, the future will take care of itself	What do you think… The police are unfair – they just pick on me for no reason
What do you think… I have never hurt someone by what I have done	What do you think… Committing crime can be a useful way of getting what you want	What do you think… The police are too violent
What do you think… Most of the stuff young people get in trouble for now is really stupid	What do you think… I will always get into trouble	What do you think… Once a criminal, always a criminal

Young People with Anti-Social Behaviours, Routledge © Kathy Hampson 2011

What do you think… There was no victim of my offences	What do you think… I can't change the way I am now	What do you think… Crime is now a way of life for me
What do you think… Committing crime is quite exciting	What do you think… I think that crime pays – it's worth it!	Who are the victims and how would they feel… *You hang around on the street corner with a big gang of mates*
Who are the victims and how would they feel… *You break a window in someone's house*	Who are the victims and how would they feel… *You graffiti on a bus shelter*	Who are the victims and how would they feel… *You make a hoax 999 call*
Who are the victims and how would they feel… *You damage some-one's garden*	Who are the victims and how would they feel… *You drop litter in the street*	Who are the victims and how would they feel… *You drop litter in the countryside*
Who are the victims and how would they feel… *You throw eggs at a house*	Who are the victims and how would they feel… *You throw a firework*	Who are the victims and how would they feel… *You stay out all night without letting anyone know*

Games 123

Who are the victims and how would they feel...

You call someone a racist name

Who are the victims and how would they feel...

You damage a parked car

Who are the victims and how would they feel...

You carry a weapon

Who are the victims and how would they feel...

You play loud music late at night

Who are the victims and how would they feel...

You are cruel to a dog

Who are the victims and how would they feel...

You drink alcohol in the street with your mates

Who are the victims and how would they feel...

You break windows in a disused building

Who are the victims and how would they feel...

You get into a stolen car

Who are the victims and how would they feel...

You take someone's mobile phone off them

Who are the victims and how would they feel...

You steal some sweets from a local shop

Who are the victims and how would they feel...

You ask to see someone's bike, and ride off on it

Who are the victims and how would they feel...

You push a smaller kid over, because they are being annoying

What do you think...

Big shops can afford to have stuff stolen from them

What do you think...

Everyone has insurance to replace their stolen stuff

What do you think...

Carrying a small knife isn't a big deal

Young People with Anti-Social Behaviours, Routledge © Kathy Hampson 2011

Self esteem

What I care about most in life is…	My friends like me because…	I like myself because…
Two of my strengths are…	The person I admire most in the world is…	The person I would most like to be is…
I have the power to…	I feel good when…	One of my best qualities is…
One of my greatest strengths is…	The best thing that could happen to me would be…	The people I like are…
The name I would like to be called is…	The sport I am best at is…	The best thing about being me is…

The most important thing in the world to me is…	I feel successful when…	What people like about me is…
If I had one super-power it would be…	I am proud of…	Two things I am good at are…
True or false… I get lots of hugs or affection from my parents/carers	True or false… I get enough attention from my parents/carers	True or false… I have someone who cares about me
True or false… I have someone who gives me praise	True or false… I feel loved	True or false… I have friends who look out for me
The person I trust the most is…	The person I care about most is…	The person who loves me the most is…

The person who makes me feel 'special' is…	The person who helps me the most is…	True or false… I feel good about myself
True or false… People care about me	The best thing that has ever happened to me is…	My best memory is…
True or false… I get praise when I have done something well	True or false… I treat people with respect	True or false… People generally treat me with respect
Name two things you do to show respect to other people	Name two things you do to show someone you are supporting them	Name two things you do to show someone you love them
Name two things you can do to make yourself feel good	Name two things you can do to cheer yourself up	Name two things you can do if you feel bored

Pot Luck

True or false… I am honest	True or false… There are people I need to say sorry to	True or false… There are things I have said or done which I regret
True or false… I wish things were different	True or false… I have people in my life who can help me	True or false… I want to make things better for myself
True or false… There are people who are afraid of me	True or false… I don't need any help	True or false… I have made mistakes in my life
Two things that make me stressed are…	True or false… I get into trouble outside	True or false… My problems are big
True or false… I blame other people for how my life has turned out	True or false… I am friendly	True or false… People like me

On a scale of 0 to 10, how good are you at taking responsibility for your own actions?	On a scale of 0 to 10, how good are you at giving respect to other people?	On a scale of 0 to 10, how good are you at looking at people when they are talking to you?
On a scale of 0 to 10, how good are you at apologizing to people when you have hurt them?	On a scale of 0 to 10, how good are you at being able to manage your temper?	On a scale of 0 to 10, how good are you at learning from your mistakes?
On a scale of 0 to 10, how easy do you find it to be affectionate to other people?	On a scale of 0 to 10, how physically aggressive are you?	On a scale of 0 to 10, how popular are you where you live?
On a scale of 0 to 10, how mature are you?	On a scale of 0 to 10, how good are you at keeping to rules?	On a scale of 0 to 10, how lazy are you?
On a scale of 0 to 10, how brave are you?	On a scale of 0 to 10, how much do you worry about your offending?	On a scale of 0 to 10, how respected are you by adults?

On a scale of 0 to 10, how happy are you with your own life?	On a scale of 0 to 10, how much of a reputation do you have as a trouble maker?	On a scale of 0 to 10, how much do you scare other people?
On a scale of 0 to 10, how worried about the future are you?	On a scale of 0 to 10, how shy are you?	On a scale of 0 to 10, how kind are you?
On a scale of 0 to 10, how well known are you to the police?	On a scale of 0 to 10, how angry are you?	On a scale of 0 to 10, how looked after do you feel?
Two things that make me happy are…	Two things that I moan about are…	Two things that worry me are…
Two things I need to change are…	Two things I remember about being at primary school are…	Two things I wish I could do are…

The consequences game (cards version)

(K/R)

This game can be played either with the following cards or read from the sheet (which is after the cards) by the facilitator, depending on what the young person would respond to best.

The method of play is the same for both formats – start with number 1, which takes you on to number 2. Beyond this, the next move depends on the decision of the young person playing. Some instructions require the flipping of a coin (when the decisions are those of others, demonstrating that we cannot always predict what others will do), so make sure there is one handy. To play using the cards, print them on sheets of card and cut up to make individual cards. The number on the front of each card must be written on the back, as they will all be laid out on the table face-down in numerical order. The young person then turns over card number 1, and the game continues from there. This helps young people to see that there is a consequence to the decisions they make.

The possible issues covered by this game are shop theft, peer pressure, bullying, fighting, weapons awareness, alcohol consumption, and criminal damage, but not all of them will feature in any given game.

1. You go with your friends to the local shop (go to 2).	**2.** One of your friends steals a comic. Do you: tell the shop keeper (go to 3), or keep quiet (go to 4)?	**3.** The shop keeper seizes hold of your friend, and calls the police. Your friend falls out with you (go to 6).
4. Next time you are in the shop, your friend dares you to steal some sweets. Do you: do it (go to 7), or refuse (go to 6)?	**5.** Your mum bans you from having anything to do with your friend. Do you: ignore her and continue seeing your friend (go to 4), or do what she says and stay away from them (go to 8)?	**6.** Your friend now falls out with you and tells everyone what you did (go to 9).

7.	8.	9.
You put a bar of chocolate in your pocket and breathe a sigh of relief when you're not caught. Do you: do it again (go to 10), or decide not to do it ever again (go to 8)?	You decide to make some new friends and start hanging round in a different group (go to 11).	Now lots of others at school have fallen out with you and are calling you names. Your original friend is spreading nasty rumours about you. Do you: have a fight with them (go to 12), or ignore them (go to 13)?
10.	11.	12.
You go back to the shop and pick up another chocolate bar to steal, only this time the shop keeper challenges you. Do you: admit what you've done (go to 14), or run away (go to 15)?	Your new friends start meeting up in the local park, but this is where your old friends hang out. Do you: make excuses not to go (go to 16), or go but keep a look out for them (go to 17)?	You catch them at lunchtime, challenge them about what they have been saying, and give them a shove. They then launch into you for a full-blown fight. They then trip you up and produce a knife from their pocket. Do you: try to get the knife off them (go to18), or yell at them to stop and not hurt you (go to 19)?

13.	14.	15.
The name calling gets so bad that you cannot just ignore it. It's really upsetting you. Do you: challenge them to a fight (go to 12), or tell an adult what's happening (go to 20)?	The shop keeper wants to call the police. Do you: swear at them (go to 21), or try to talk them round (go to 22)?	You get back home having run all the way from the shop, and your mum asks you why you're so out of breath. Do you: admit what you've done (go to 23), or tell her some story about jogging to keep fit (go to 24)?
16.	17.	18.
Your new friends go to the park without you, and you start to feel left out. Do you: go along with them eventually (go to 17), or try to persuade them to hang out somewhere else (go to 25)?	You are at the park with your new friends, but see a group of your old friends coming towards you. Do you: ignore them and try to pretend you haven't seen them (go to 26), or acknowledge them when they get up to you, and say 'hi' (go to 27)?	They panic and slash out at your hand with the knife. You are in extreme pain, and there is blood everywhere. The other person looks on, horrified, and runs away. Do you: get someone to get help (go to 28), or wrap up your hand in your jumper and hope it stops bleeding (go to 29)?

Young People with Anti-Social Behaviours, Routledge © Kathy Hampson 2011

19. They put the knife back in their pocket and threaten you that they will get you if you tell anyone about it. Do you: tell an adult about the knife (go to 30), or keep quiet about it (go to 31)?

20. You are not sure whether to tell your mum, or tell someone at school. What is going to make it stop? Do you: tell your mum (go to 32), or tell a teacher (go to 33)?

21. The shop keeper gets really annoyed, and grabs hold of you while they call the police. When the police arrive, they arrest you for shop lifting and for using threatening and abusive language to the shop keeper.

GAME OVER!

22 The shop keeper eventually calms down and says that he won't call the police as long as you never go in their shop again. You agree.

GAME OVER

23. Your mum marches you back to the shop to apologize to the shop keeper. Do you: apologize and stay polite (go to 22), or refuse to apologize and swear at them instead (go to 21)?

24. Your mum believes you, thank goodness! After a while, you forget about it and end up back in the shop, this time with your mum. The shop keeper recognizes you and tells your mum that you stole a chocolate bar from his shop, but then ran away. Do you: deny it, and say they are lying (go to 25), or admit it to your mum and apologize to the shop keeper (go to 22)?

Young People with Anti-Social Behaviours, Routledge © Kathy Hampson 2011

25.	26.	27.
The shop keeper says that actually they have you on their CCTV in the act of theft, and now they are going to call the police, as they can identify you. The police arrest you for shop theft.

GAME OVER! | Your old friends see you and start asking you what you're doing and whether you want to go to a party with them tonight. Do you: chat to them but say you can't go out (go to 34), or agree to meet them tonight for the party (go to 35)? | When you start chatting, they ask you to come to a party tonight. Do you: chat to them but say you can't go out (go to 34), or agree to meet them tonight for the party (go to 35)? |
| 28. | 29. | 30. |
| Someone hears you calling for help and comes to see what the problem is. They look horrified, and ask you if you want them to call an ambulance. Do you: think you will be in too much trouble if they do, so you won't agree and say it'll be ok (go to 29), or do you know that you are seriously injured, so agree (go to 36)? | You find somewhere to hide out until your hand stops bleeding, but it won't. Do you: not dare to look at it, just bind it up tighter – it's bound to stop bleeding soon (go to 37), or realize you are seriously hurt and ring for an ambulance (go to 36)? | You find a member of staff and report that this person has a knife. They have their pockets searched by the police. Do they: find a knife (heads) (go to 37), not find a knife (tails) (go to 38)? [Flip a coin to decide.] |

31.	32.	33.
You don't tell anyone about the knife, but hear later on that they threatened a young child with it. Do you: report the knife now before someone gets hurt (go to 30), or still keep quiet, because it's not your problem (go to 39)?	Your mum rings up the school to report the bullying issue. The head teacher hauls the bully in and warns them to stop. Do they: stop (heads) (go to 40), or carry on (tails) (go to 9)? [Flip a coin to decide.]	The teacher passes on what is happening to the head teacher, who hauls the bully in and warns them to stop. Do they: stop (heads) (go to 40), or carry on (tails) (go to 9)? [Flip a coin to decide.]
34. You stay with your new friendship group, and decide to go out with them to the cinema instead. GAME OVER!	**35.** You meet them later that evening. They have lots of alcohol, and offer you some. Do you: drink it (go to 41), or refuse it (go to 42)?	**36.** You are taken to hospital by ambulance. You need several stitches in your hand, and you have serious ligament damage. They dress your hand after stitching, and tell you that you may not be able to write with it again. GAME OVER!

Young People with Anti-Social Behaviours, Routledge © Kathy Hampson 2011

37.	38.	39.
You start to feel really faint, and wonder what to do. Your hand continues to bleed. A lot. Do you: get someone to ring for an ambulance (go to 43), or pass out (go to 44)?	The police do not find a knife, but they warn the person that they will be keeping an eye on them. Do they: take this warning seriously and leave you alone (heads) (go to 40), or ignore this warning and come to find you (tails) (go to 45)? [Flip a coin to decide.]	Several days later this person is involved in another fight, but this time used the knife, and killed the person. You never reported it. GAME OVER!
40.	41.	42.
Your life gets back on track, and you get involved with new friends. GAME OVER!	You drink the alcohol they give you, and start to feel giddy. They walk along the road hitting car wing mirrors off as they go. Do you: join in (go to 46), or give some excuses and leave (go to 47)?	You start walking along with your friends to the party, but they are getting very rowdy and start knocking the wing mirrors off cars as they go. Do you: go along with it (go to 46), or give some excuses and leave (go to 47)?

43.	44.	45.
The ambulance rushes you to hospital, where you need several stitches and a blood transfusion because of the extreme blood loss you have suffered, and are told you have such bad ligament damage that you may not be able to write again. GAME OVER!	You're dead! GAME OVER!	The person jumps out at you when you are walking home by yourself, and produces the knife again. They lunge at you saying, 'This is for grassing on me.' You protect your face with your hand, and it is badly lacerated. They run off and leave you bleeding on the ground (go to 28).
46.	**47.**	**48.**
You all carry on walking, making rather a lot of noise, when a police car comes round the corner. Do you: run away (go to 48), or stay where you are (go to 49)?	You realize you were right first time when you decided not to hang around with them anymore, and go back to being with the new friends you made. GAME OVER!	The police pour out of the car and run after you. Do you: get caught (go to 49), or get away (go to 50)?

49. The police arrest you for criminal damage and being drunk and disorderly. You are locked up, interviewed, and bailed to appear in court. GAME OVER!	50. You get away and manage to go home. Some days later, the police come and arrest you, as you have been caught on CCTV with the group vandalizing cars. Someone also gave your name. GAME OVER!

THE CONSEQUENCES GAME (A)

(To be read to the young person.)

1. You go with your friends to the local shop (go to 2).

2. One of your friends steals a comic. Do you: tell the shop keeper (go to 3), or keep quiet (go to 4)?

3. The shop keeper seizes hold of your friend, and calls the police. Your friend falls out with you (go to 6).

4. Next time you are in the shop, your friend dares you to steal some sweets. Do you: do it (go to 7), or refuse (go to 6)?

5. Your mum bans you from having anything to do with your friend. Do you: ignore her and continue seeing your friend (go to 4), or do what she says and stay away from them (go to 8)?

6. Your friend now falls out with you and tells everyone what you did (go to 9).

7. You put a bar of chocolate in your pocket and breathe a sigh of relief when you're not caught. Do you: do it again (go to 10), or decide not to do it ever again (go to 8)?

8. You decide to make some new friends and start hanging round in a different group (go to 11).

9. Now lots of others at school have fallen out with you and are calling you names. Your original friend is spreading nasty rumours about you. Do you: have a fight with them (go to 12), or ignore them (go to 13)?

10. You go back to the shop and pick up another chocolate bar to steal, only this time the shop keeper challenges you. Do you: admit what you've done (go to 14), or run away (go to 15)?

11. Your new friends start meeting up in the local park, but this is where your old friends hang out. Do you: make excuses not to go (go to 16), or go but keep a look out for them (go to 17)?

12. You catch them at lunchtime, challenge them about what they have been saying, and give them a shove. They then launch into you for a full-blown fight. They then trip you up and produce a knife from their pocket. Do you: try to get the knife off them (go to18), or yell at them to stop and not hurt you (go to 19)?

13. The name calling gets so bad that you cannot just ignore it. It's really upsetting you. Do you: challenge them to a fight (go to 12), or tell an adult what's happening (go to 20)?

14. The shop keeper wants to call the police. Do you: swear at them (go to 21), or try to talk them round (go to 22)?

15. You get back home having run all the way from the shop, and your mum asks you why you're so out of breath. Do you: admit what you've done (go to 23), or tell her some story about jogging to keep fit (go to 24)?

16. Your new friends go to the park without you, and you start to feel left out. Do you: go along with them eventually (go to 17), or try to persuade them to hang out somewhere else (go to 25)?

17. You are at the park with your new friends, but see a group of your old friends coming towards you. Do you: ignore them and try to pretend you haven't seen them (go to 26), or acknowledge them when they get up to you, and say 'hi' (go to 27)?

18. They panic and slash out at your hand with the knife. You are in extreme pain, and there is blood everywhere. The other person looks on, horrified, and runs away. Do you: get someone to get help (go to 28), or wrap up your hand in your jumper and hope it stops bleeding (go to 29)?

19. They put the knife back in their pocket and threaten you that they will get you if you tell anyone about it. Do you: tell an adult about the knife (go to 30), or keep quiet about it (go to 31)?

20. You are not sure whether to tell your mum, or tell someone at school. What is going to make it stop? Do you: tell your mum (go to 32), or tell a teacher (go to 33)?

21. The shop keeper gets really annoyed, and grabs hold of you while they call the police. When the police arrive, they arrest you for shop lifting and for using threatening and abusive language to the shop keeper. **GAME OVER!**

22. The shop keeper eventually calms down and says that he won't call the police as long as you never go in their shop again. You agree. GAME OVER!

23. Your mum marches you back to the shop to apologize to the shop keeper. Do you: apologize and stay polite (go to 22), or refuse to apologize and swear at them instead (go to 21)?

24. Your mum believes you, thank goodness! After a while, you forget about it and end up back in the shop, this time with your mum. The shop keeper recognizes you and says to your mum that you stole a chocolate bar from his shop, but then ran away. Do you: deny it, and say they are lying (go to 25), or admit it to your mum and apologize to the shop keeper (go to 22)?

25. The shop keeper says that actually they have you on their CCTV in the act of theft, and now they are going to call the police, as they can identify you. The police arrest you for shop theft. GAME OVER!

26. Your old friends see you and start asking you what you're doing and whether you want to go to a party with them tonight. Do you: chat to them but say you can't go out (go to 34), or agree to meet them tonight for the party (go to 35)?

27. When you start chatting, they ask you to come to a party tonight. Do you: chat to them but say you can't go out (go to 34), or agree to meet them tonight for the party (go to 35)?

28. Someone hears you calling for help and comes to see what the problem is. They look horrified, and ask you if you want them to call an ambulance. Do you: think you will be in too much trouble if they do, so you won't agree and say it'll be ok (go to 29), or do you know that you are seriously injured, so agree (go to 36)?

29. You find somewhere to hide out until your hand stops bleeding, but it won't. Do you: not dare to look at it, just bind it up tighter – it's bound to stop bleeding soon (go to 37), or realize you are seriously hurt and ring for an ambulance (go to 36)?

30. You find a member of staff and report that this person has a knife. They have their pockets searched by the police. Do they: find a knife (heads) (go to 37), not find a knife (tails) (go to 38)? (Flip a coin to decide.)

31. You don't tell anyone about the knife, but hear later on that they threatened a young child with it. Do you: report the knife now before someone gets hurt (go to 30), or still keep quiet, because it's not your problem (go to 39)?

32. Your mum rings up the school to report the bullying issue. The head teacher hauls the bully in and warns them to stop. Do they: stop (heads) (go to 40), or carry on (tails) (go to 9)? (Flip a coin to decide.)

33. The teacher passes on what is happening to the head teacher, who hauls the bully in and warns them to stop. Do they: stop (heads) (go to 40), or carry on (tails) (go to 9)? (Flip a coin to decide.)

34. You stay with your new friendship group, and decide to go out with them to the cinema instead. GAME OVER!

35. You meet them later that evening. They have lots of alcohol, and offer you some. Do you: drink it (go to 41), or refuse it (go to 42)?

36. You are taken to hospital by ambulance. You need several stitches in your hand, and you have serious ligament damage. They dress your hand after stitching, and tell you that you may not be able to write with it again. GAME OVER!

37. You start to feel really faint, and wonder what to do. Your hand continues to bleed. A lot. Do you: get someone to ring for an ambulance (go to 43), or pass out (go to 44)?

38. The police do not find a knife, but they warn the person that they will be keeping an eye on them. Do they: take this warning seriously and leave you alone (heads) (go to 40), or ignore this warning and come to find you (tails) (go to 45)? (Flip a coin to decide.)

39. Several days later this person is involved in another fight, but this time used the knife, and killed the person. You never reported it. GAME OVER!

40. Your life gets back on track, and you get involved with new friends. GAME OVER!

41. You drink the alcohol they give you, and start to feel giddy. They walk along the road hitting car wing mirrors off as they go. Do you: join in (go to 46), or give some excuses and leave (go to 47)?

42. You start walking along with your friends to the party, but they are getting very rowdy and start knocking the wing mirrors off cars as they go. Do you: go along with it (go to 46), or give some excuses and leave (go to 47)?

43. The ambulance rushes you to hospital, where you need several stitches and a blood transfusion because of the extreme blood loss you have suffered, and are told you have such bad ligament damage that you may not be able to write again. GAME OVER!

44. You're dead! GAME OVER!

45. The person jumps out at you when you are walking home by yourself, and produces the knife again. They lunge at you saying, 'This is for grassing on me.' You protect your face with your hand, and it is badly lacerated. They run off and leave you bleeding on the ground (go to 28).

46. You all carry on walking, making rather a lot of noise, when a police car comes round the corner. Do you: run away (go to 48), or stay where you are (go to 49)?

47. You realize you were right first time when you decided not to hang around with them anymore, and go back to being with the new friends you made. GAME OVER!

48. The police pour out of the car and run after you. Do you: get caught (go to 49), or get away (go to 50)?

49. The police arrest you for criminal damage and being drunk and disorderly. You are locked up, interviewed, and bailed to appear in court. GAME OVER!

50. You get away and manage to go home. Some days later, the police come and arrest you, as you have been caught on CCTV with the group vandalizing cars. Someone also gave your name. GAME OVER!

A year in the life (V/A/R/K)

(With thanks to Hayley Pearson for her contribution to this game.)

This is a simple board game played with playing pieces and a die (the playing pieces can be anything of a reasonable size to fit on the board spaces). There are three sets of cards: anti-social behaviour cards, pro-social behaviour cards, and wild cards (which need to be printed out on different colour card and cut into individual cards). The board is designed to be printed out onto four A4 pages, and then fixed together to make a large playing surface.

The game takes the players through the seasons of the year (it is very important that the board sections are fixed together in the correct order: Winter is the start and goes top left, spring goes top right, summer goes bottom right, and autumn is the end, going bottom left).

When a player lands on a dark grey space, they pick up an anti-social behaviour card and read it out. There are consequences to the action on the card, which can be avoided by identifying who would be affected by the action and how they might feel about it. If they successfully avoid the consequence, then they stay on that space until their next turn. Cards are replaced at the bottom of the pack for use again should the game go beyond one run through the cards (but the mitigation has to be different if the card is used again for the consequence to be avoided again). Please note that some of these cards are seasonal, so should be placed at a logical position in the pack (for example, the ones about snow and ice should be at the beginning because that is the winter section).

When a player lands on a light grey space, they take a pro-social behaviour card and read it out. They can double up their reward if they can identify a reason why the action is good or beneficial, and who might benefit (discretion is with the facilitator to accept or decline the explanations). If they move forward as a result and land on an anti-social behaviour space, they do not have to take an anti-social behaviour card, and their turn ends.

When a player lands on a space with W, they take a wild card, and read it out. These are moral quandary situations, in which they have to decide what they would do. The facilitator can judge what they get for this based on how acceptable behaviour-wise the answer is. They can make them go up to three spaces back, or allow them to go up to three spaces forward. This might depend on how legal their suggestion is, how much empathy it shows for others, or how much awareness of social norms they demonstrate.

The winner is the player who gets to the finish square first, but they do not need to land on it exactly. Throwing a six does NOT secure a second throw!

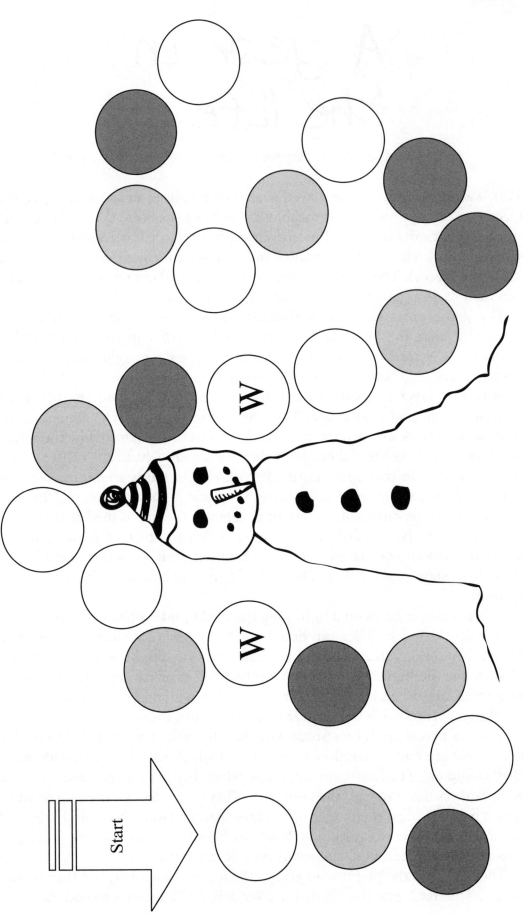

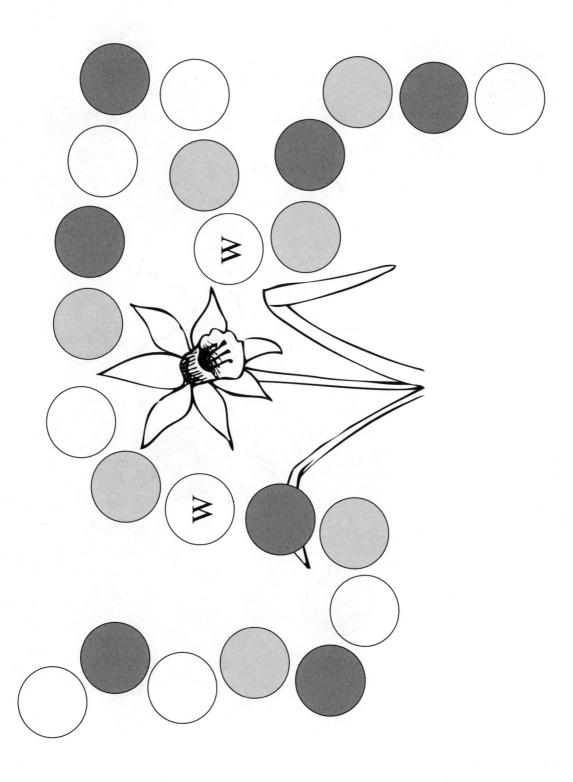

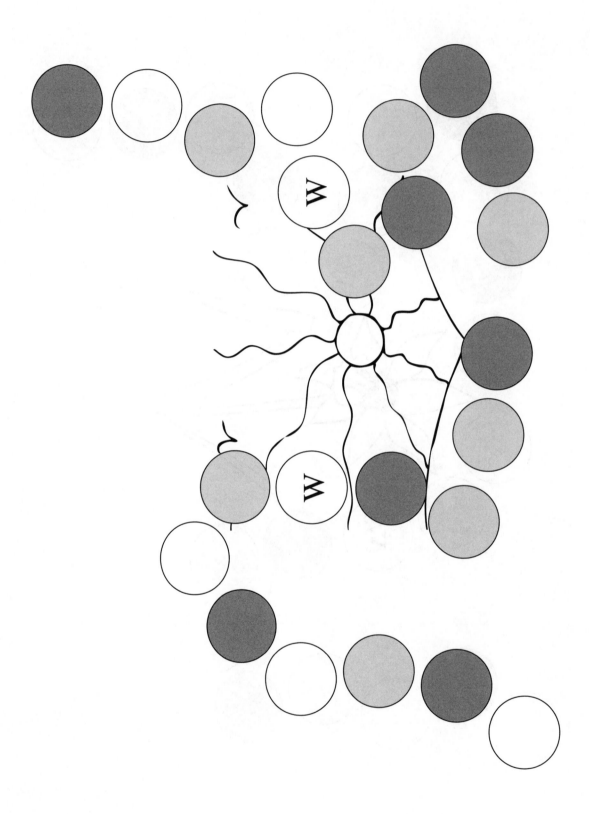

Anti-social behaviour cards (dark grey spot)

You break the window in a bus Miss a go	You trip someone up in the street Go back two spaces
You throw a snowball at someone's house, cracking a window Go back three spaces	You play a game lobbing a snowball through someone's open door Miss a go
You make a black ice strip in the pavement Go back two spaces	You throw a snowball at a passing car Miss a go
You have drunk too much, and fell over when going home, twisting your ankle Go back one space	You and a friend decide to go for a joy ride in a digger around the building site Go back four spaces
You come in two hours later than your mum wanted you home, but hadn't told her where you were Miss a go	You and your friends wrote your names on a bus shelter Go back two spaces

You throw an egg at someone's house because she'd told you off the previous day Miss a go	You and your friends creep into a garden shed that happens to be open, and take the football that is on the floor Go back three spaces
You are bored, so ring 999 just for the buzz Miss two goes	You and your friend break the vodka bottle on the pavement when it is finished, leaving the glass in shards Go back four places
You spit your chewing gum out onto the pavement when you are fed up with it Go back one space	You spit on the pavement Go back one space
You steal some apples from a tree in a nearby garden Go back two spaces	You and your friends go garage hopping Miss a go
You find a wheelie bin in the street and set the rubbish inside on fire Go back four spaces	You drop your chip papers on the ground when you are finished with them Go back one space
You throw a firework at one of your mates Go back five spaces	You nick a bike off a kid in the street and go for a ride around the neighbourhood Go back two spaces

Young People with Anti-Social Behaviours, Routledge © Kathy Hampson 2011

Pro-social behaviour cards (light grey spot)

You wash up for your mum Go forward two spaces	You make your mum a cup of tea without being asked Go forward one space
You attend school for a whole month without a day off Go forward two spaces	You decide to go swimming with your friends Go forward one space
You and your friends play football in the local park Go forward one space	You work well in school all week Go forward two spaces
You help a neighbour with their garden Go forward three spaces	You tidy your room Go forward two spaces
You sort your own washing out, wash it, and put it out to dry Go forward two spaces	You make a cake Go forward one space

You get a good school report Go forward three places	You come in on time every night for a month Go forward three spaces
You take the dog out for a walk without being asked Go forward one space	You cook tea for your whole family Go forward three spaces
You befriend someone at school who was being picked on Go forward three spaces	You get all your homework done without moaning or putting it off Go forward two spaces
You share sweets with other young people who come round Go forward one space	You run an errand to the local shop on the first time of being asked Go forward two spaces
You make a round of toast for everyone Go forward one space	You vacuum up the living room because it needs it, not because you were asked! Go forward two spaces

Wild cards

You find a wallet in the street, which has inside it the address and ID of the owner, several credit cards, and a photo of a child. It also has £30 inside. What do you do?	You meet up with some friends and one of them offers you a really nice mobile phone for £10. What do you do?
Your little brother comes home from school crying because he has been picked on by a bigger kid in the next street. What do you do?	You see two young people climbing into the window of a house in your street. What do you do?
You are in your local corner shop buying some chocolate, and notice that the shop keeper, who has been chatting to you, has given you too much change. What do you do?	You are with a friend in a shop in town. They slip something in their pocket, and ask you to carry it out in case a store detective saw them picking it up. What do you do?
Your friend hands you a cannabis spliff to share with them. What do you do?	Your friend gives you a small bag of cannabis that they are carrying, saying that they need you to save it for them. What do you do?
Your friend roars up to you on a motorbike you've never seen before. You're pretty sure it isn't theirs, but they ask you to hop on the back. What do you do?	You see a young person you vaguely know carrying a large TV down an alleyway. He asks you to help him. What do you do?

Young People with Anti-Social Behaviours, Routledge © Kathy Hampson 2011

Part 4

Group Sessions

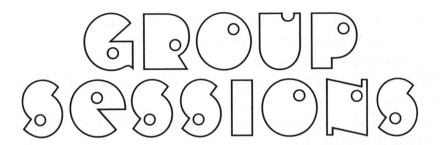

Introduction

The group sessions in this section cover a variety of anti-social behaviour issues including peer pressure, alcohol and drugs, bullying, criminal damage, racism, truancy, and fighting. They are designed for a wide range of groups, from youth inclusion projects, youth offending teams and youth groups, through to schools and colleges, each one including a range of learning styles to hold attention.

The structure of this section aims to make running a group as easy as possible, with a range of ice-breakers, games to mix up groups, and end games from which facilitators can choose to make the group as appropriate to their particular young people as possible. These can then be added to the single-sheet session plans, which should be copied for the facilitators to refer to throughout the session in progress. Fuller explanations of each exercise are made before each plan. Spaces have also been left on the session plans for facilitators to add the names or initials of who will be leading each section. It is recommended that there are at least two facilitators, as this aids group dynamics, enables a variety of voices and styles for each session, and helps the discipline side of small group facilitation.

Groups usually work best when they are in a circle formation, so try to get the young people into some sort of circle, if the venue allows.

Group contract

It is important to begin, however briefly, with an agreement about acceptable behaviour during sessions. This enables participants to feel safe, and helps in matters of discipline. Best practice is that the young people themselves decide what they would like to include, although they may need some suggestions to begin with. I suggest writing all agreed ground rules for groups on a piece of flipchart paper, which is stuck on the wall during the group (and any subsequent ones involving the same participants). Try to write up suggestions in a positive way (dos rather than don'ts), even if they are given to you phrased negatively.

The group facilitators need to decide what they want to do beforehand about infringements of agreed rules, so they feel equipped to challenge disruptive or unhelpful behaviour, preferably away from the group situation.

Here are some suggestions for useful ground rules:

- Respect each other (discuss what you mean by respect).
- Turn off mobile phones (or put onto silent).
- It is ok not to say anything.
- Let each person finish what they are saying before someone else speaks.
- Come to the group on time.
- Everything said in the group stays in the group (confidentiality).
- Speak nicely to each other.
- It is ok to disagree with something someone says, but they have a right to say it.

Don't spend too long on this, but make sure everyone knows what is expected of them. This saves unexpected problems later on.

Ice-breaker games

Here is a selection of ice-breaker games. It is important not to miss out breaking the ice, thinking it may be a waste of time, because it allows people to say something in the group setting that is unimportant, meaning they are much more likely to be able to speak when discussions become more challenging. It also allows for introductions in groups of people who may not know each other, and a chance to learn each other's names.

There are many books of ice-breakers on the market, or available free on the internet, should you want further suggestions.

Glove game

Put some water in a surgical glove (or two together, if you are not confident about their strength!) and tie it at the top. Throw the glove around to members of the group, each person receiving it saying their name, and their favourite food. This can then be done again (possibly with people saying the name of the person to whom they are throwing it), but this time people say a food they would not eat even if they had a gun to their head!

Ball-throwing

Using a light ball (hand sized, or slightly larger), throw it around the group, with each person saying their name and some other response to a question (for example, what super power they would like to have, what crazy ambition they have, what they would do if they won £1 million).

Alliterative names

Going round the circle, each person says their name and a describing word beginning with the same letter (or sound), for example Daring David, Bonny Becky.

Surprising facts

Going round the circle, each person says their name and one surprising fact about themselves that they think no one knows.

Two truths and a lie

Each person says two things that are true about themselves and one that is a lie. The group has to identify the lie.

Fact guessing

Each person writes on a piece of paper one fact about themselves, which is then folded and put into a hat or other receptacle The hat is then passed round with each person drawing out a fact and trying to guess who wrote it.

I am going to the seaside

The facilitator begins this by saying, 'I am going to the seaside and I'm taking...', finishing the sentence with something that the person to their left is wearing. The turn then passes to the right, with the next person saying the sentence and trying to finish it. The facilitator tells them each time whether they can go or not. The object is for the participants to guess what the condition on the items to take is, and therefore getting it correct. This can take as long as the facilitators let it take! Have a time limit in mind.

Wink murder

One member of the group goes out of the room. While they are out, the group chooses a murderer who kills people by winking at them. The 'detective' comes back in and tries to decide, by watching people 'die', who is doing the killing. This is more effective if people stand up, allowing for some dramatic deaths!

Charades

Each person is given a piece of paper on which there is the name of a film, book, or TV programme, which they have to communicate to the rest of the group just by miming.

Animals

Everyone in turn around the group finishes the sentence, 'If I was an animal I would be...'.

Odd objects

Have a collection of weird, wonderful, and varied objects in the middle of the group space. Each person selects an object they feel says something about them and, going round the group, says why they chose that particular one.

Phobias

Using the phobias listed below, or finding some other ones if need be, copy both the phobia and the identification of that phobia on to separate cards, then get the group to match them up, by having the possible answers spread out in the middle of the group. This could be done as a whole group exercise, or by giving each individual a different phobia to decide on. This could also be played as a mix-up game by giving the phobias to one half of the group, and what they mean to the other half and get them to find their other half!

Beards – Pogonophobia
Dreams – Oneirophobia
Friday the 13th – Paraskavedekatriaphobia
Chins – Geniophobia
Mushrooms – Mycophobia
Belly buttons – Omphalophobia
Worms – Scoleciphobia
Gravity – Barophobia
Creepy, crawly things – Herpetophobia
Bogeyman – Bogyphobia
Mirrors – Catoptrophobia
Fish – Ichthyophobia
Nosebleeds – Epistaxiophobia
Dogs – Cynophobia
Hands – Chirophobia
Razors – Xyrophobia
Flowers – Anthrophobia
String – Linonophobia
Kissing – Philemaphobia
Dancing – Chorophobia
Frogs – Batrachophobia
Work – Ergophobia
Peanut butter sticking to the roof of the mouth – Arachibutyrophobia
Puppets – Pupaphobia
Chickens – Alektorophobia
Ghosts – Phasmophobia

Mix-up games

During a group, it might be desirable to mix up the order in which people are sitting so as to break up cliques, encourage talk with new people, or stimulate different types of discussion. Although this may be indicated at various points during a session, it may be something that is best left to specific group facilitators to decide to use as appropriate.

As before, there are other books with more game suggestions and, as always, an internet search should yield some interesting possibilities.

Birth months

Each member of the group finds others in the group with the same birth month. They then sit down with others born in the same month, working round the group from January to December.

Stand up if...

The facilitator says, 'Stand up if...', finishing with suggestions such as 'you prefer Eastenders to Coronation Street', 'you prefer McDonalds to Burger King', or 'you prefer Coca-Cola to Pepsi'. When people are standing up in response, they then have to swap places with someone else who is standing. This can be done until the facilitators are happy with the seating positions in the group.

Animal noises

Facilitators give a small piece of paper to each participant with the name of an animal written on it (this requires at least two of each animal). They have to find their pair or group by making the animal noise only (no words, no miming, and make sure the pieces of paper are not visible!) They then have to sit with their group or pair in the circle.

The farm

All group participants are labelled a cow, sheep, pig or chicken. One person then stands in the middle and their chair is taken away. They call out one of the four animals, and those labelled as such have to get up and take the chair of someone else also standing up, but the person in the middle has to try to steal a chair space, or they are in the middle again. The person then left in the middle is the caller. As well as saying individual animals, they can call out two at once, or say 'farmyard', at which everyone has to get up and swap places while trying not to let the caller get a seat.

Heights

The group have to get themselves into height order completely silently! They then sit in height order around the group.

Birthdays

The group have to get themselves into birthday order (can be just day and month rather than year), but they can speak to do this. They then sit according to the order they have constructed.

Alphabet

This requires the group to know each other's names reasonably well, and be literate. They get themselves into alphabetical order according to first name without speaking, and then sit in order.

Colours of the rainbow

Each person has a small piece of paper and a pen on which they write one of the colours of the rainbow (go through them if necessary). They then pass their paper to the person on their left. They then put themselves in rainbow order according to the colour on the paper they have been given by their neighbour.

Swaps

The facilitator announces 'all those... swap places'. Possibilities for the gap: who were born in May, who have a cat, who have a dog, who have been to America, who like chocolate, who are afraid of spiders, who have a brother... the possibilities are endless!

Celebrities

Collect some pictures of famous celebrities and put them in the middle of the floor. All participants choose a picture, then say what they like or don't like about that person. Afterwards they put themselves into alphabetical order according to the surname of the celebrities. (This can also be played as an ice-breaker, without the end part.)

End games

These provide a good way to round off sessions, allowing a wind-down if the subject matter has proved challenging, sometimes helping participants to identify points of learning from the session.

Name and learning

Go round the group, starting with a volunteer, who decides which way round the circle or room to go, with each person saying their name (if they do not know each other very well) and one thing they have learnt from the session.

Emotions

Put different emotions on cards (possibly using emotions from the emotions cards – see page 00 – and have some repeated ones) which are put in the middle of the room. Each person chooses a card that represents something about what they are feeling.

Sweeties

Pass round a box of wrapped chocolates or sweets, with each person selecting one, and saying one thing they have learnt from the session.

Appreciation

Put some sweets (wrapped), or some other reward items like quirky stickers in the middle of the floor. Each person selects one and gives it to another group member, whilst saying one thing they have appreciated about them. Ensure that each person can only receive one item!

Ball/glove

As in the ice-breaker games, throw a water-filled glove, or a small soft ball around the group, with each person saying one thing of relevance from the session.

Plastic animals

Buy a set of plastic animals (farm, wild, or even dinosaurs!), put them in the centre of the room and ask each person to select one they can relate to. Each person then says why they chose that particular one. Group facilitators need to decide in advance whether group members can keep the animals or whether they need to put them back!

New facts

The glove (or ball) is thrown around, with each person saying one new fact they have learnt about the person to whom they throw it.

Aliens

The ball or glove is passed round, with each person saying one thing they think an alien would think about the human race if they came to Earth for a day.

Remote control

Using a remote control vehicle of some kind, one group member steers the vehicle to another group member, who then gets the controls and has to steer it towards another group member, until it has been once to every group member.

Paper aeroplanes

Give each group member a piece of A4 paper, and tell them to make a paper plane. Conclude with a competition to see whose goes furthest.

The junk game

This is a group game that can be played for a variety of different purposes, depending on the issues involved. If the purpose is to improve the participants' empathy for others, use the empathy scenario cards from the empathy game on page 00. If the purpose is to concentrate on the consequences of behaviour, then use the cards with specific anti-social behaviours; see page 00.

Materials needed

A large amount of junk – discarded bottles, boxes, packaging that can be stacked in some way other than flat.
Sticky tape per team.
The question cards being used.

Method

This is a team game, so split the participants into teams, depending on how many there are.

The purpose for each team is to build the highest tower with the junk; the purpose for the facilitator is to encourage the participants to actively think about the scenarios being used.

The game begins with one of the team members responding to one of the cards. If these are the empathy cards, then they have to think either of an appropriate emotion that person might feel, or a thought they might have – the facilitator can use their discretion as to whether the emotions card can be used, or whether an emotion can only be used once by each team. If the anti-social behaviour cards are being used, then they have to think of a consequence of that action. Alternatively, they could think who might be a victim. If they give an appropriate response they choose a piece of junk, which they put on the floor in front of their team. The turn then moves to another team, who then take their turn. The game moves around the teams, with each team member taking their turn (or alternatively it could be a group response, depending on capabilities).

The game continues until the cards are completed (the facilitator needs to ensure there are enough cards for an even number of turns per team). The teams are then given a fixed amount of time in which to build the highest tower with their junk (sticky tape can be used in construction, if the facilitator allows). The winners are the team with the highest tower.

Burglary

Ground rules discussion.

Opening game: choose an opening game from the selection.

Burglary experience

Put your hand up if… (and don't take it down until the exercise has finished):

You have been burgled.
Anyone in your family has been burgled.
Anyone in your street has been burgled.
Anyone you know has been burgled.

As you can see, burglary affects the vast majority of people in some way. No one is immune, and no one is completely unaffected.

Statistics

Present the following statistics from the British Crime Survey 2007/8 (update these statistics from the internet by searching for the survey), which could be discussed according to their expectations, or by asking the young people to guess the facts and numbers, possibly using a multiple choice of suggestions for the answer.

> *According to the British Crime Survey 2007/8, there were 729,000 burglaries committed in the preceding year in Britain (this is a fall from the peak of 1,770,000 in 1995). Only 64 per cent of burglaries were reported to the police, and 2.4 per cent of all households reported in that survey being a victim of burglary during that year. Households with no security measures in their home were 10 times more likely to be a victim of burglary than those with security measures like window locks, alarms, etc. (Crime in England and Wales 2007/8, by Kershaw, Nicholas and Walker, 2008, Home Office)*

Emotions

Put an array of emotions written on cards on the floor for people to choose.

Every participant chooses an emotion that they think they would feel if they were burgled. Going round the group, preferably beginning with a volunteer, each person says what they have chosen and why. This gives a chance for people who have been affected by burglary to share something, but also to say something less personal if they do not want to share.

Imagination role-play

Ask the participants to close their eyes and relax, and read through the following piece of writing, slowly and expressively:

> *It's a lovely day and you have been out all afternoon with your mates in town. Your mum said she would be home late today, so would you please make sure the washing up had been done. Ah, that means you can have the place to yourself for a while – excellent! You walk up to your door and notice some bits of plastic strewn in the way. That's odd, you think. I wonder who left that there. You are about the put your key in the door to unlock it, when the door swings open... you see inside... the floor is littered with objects. It is then that you see the lock on the door has been forced... you've been burgled. You have a sudden thought... are they still there in house? What did they use to get the door open? Are they armed? You creep through the door and into the first room. The floor is again covered with the contents of some of the drawers and cupboards. There's mess everywhere. The TV is gone, along with the CD player and the laptop. Oh no... that had all your GCSE work on it. What are you going to do about that? It needs to be handed in soon. You then realize that they could have gone in your bedroom and you rush up the stairs to see. Your heart sinks when you see your door open and the contents of your cupboard trailing out of the room. They've ransacked the place, taken your MP3 player, AND the CDs loaded onto it. They also appear to have taken your favourite trainers and jeans. Your mind whizzes round now to think what else could be missing.*

Before you move on, ask for general responses about how participating in that exercise made the participants feel.

Word shower consequences

Having got the participants to imagine being in a situation where they have experienced a burglary, use the following exercise to investigate a little more how it may affect them. Using a flipchart, ask for responses from the group about the things they would be most upset about losing in a burglary, and write them on one half of the paper. On the other half ask for and write the responses to what they would be most upset about if they were burgled (they might say the feeling of intrusion, the damage or the mess, or a feeling of powerlessness).

Why does it happen? Ask participants to think why people might burgle a house, and put the responses on the flipchart. Try to encourage them to be as imaginative as possible and include different motivations for needing some money, for example, drug or alcohol addiction, being in poverty themselves, wanting specific items they cannot afford and so on.

What do you think about them? Ask all the participants to think of one word to describe what they think about young people who burgle houses (they may have a more balanced view after the previous discussion), and go round the circle with everyone giving their response.

This will be off-putting to those within the group who have committed burglaries, who will hear negative opinions given, and may dissuade those tempted from following through. It relies on some pro-social peer pressure from the group as a whole, so you may need to do this slightly differently if the group is likely to give anti-social responses (for example, you can talk instead about the consequences they think are likely for those caught for burglary, and make a list of those instead).

End game

Choose an end game from the selection.

Group session plan: burglary

Exercise time	Total time	Exercise	Items needed	Facilitator
3 mins	3 mins	Ground rules	Flipchart Pens	
5 mins	8 mins	Opening game		
2 mins	10 mins	Burglary experience – Hand up if... You have been burgled Anyone in your family has been burgled Anyone in your street has been burgled Anyone you know has been burgled It affects us all….		
5 mins	15 mins	Statistics		
10 mins	25 mins	Emotions – choose an emotion from the floor they would feel if burgled	Emotions cards	
5 mins	30 mins	Imagination role-play – read the story out to the group as they close their eyes and relax. How did that make you feel?	Story	
10 mins	40 mins	Word shower consequences – Two questions from which to flipchart responses: What would you be most upset to lose? What would most upset you about being burgled?	Flipchart Pens	
10 mins	50 mins	Why does it happen? Flipchart why young people burgle.	Flipchart Pens	
5 mins	55 mins	What do you think about them?		
5 mins	60 mins	End game		

Alcohol

Ground rules discussion.

Opening game: choose an opening game from the selection.

What do you know?

Have the group form a circle. Distribute the alcohol fact or fiction cards (see page 72) around the group (if there are too many group members, pair them up and give them one between two). Place the large True/Not true response cards from page 00 (preferably printed on coloured paper and laminated) in the middle of the circle. Starting with a volunteer, each participant reads out their card and then says whether they think it is true or false, placing it on the appropriate response card. If you feel that the group will be supportive enough, allow some discussion on whether other group members agree with their decision, also probing into their reasons. If you feel the group would be too critical of each other, wait until all the cards have been used and then have a group discussion about where each card should go and why.

Mix-up game

Choose a mix-up game from the selection that will mix up the group and preferably put people in groups (or count off into groups according to where they are now sitting).

Alcohol ethics

Using the newly arranged groups, give each group a card containing one of the following ethical situations (it doesn't matter if more than one group looks at the same situation):

It's ok to drive if I've only had a couple of drinks. I know I'm fine!

It's good fun to see how much friends can drink before they throw up. I dared my friend to drink the whole vodka bottle... he was fine!

I would spike a friend's drink with vodka without telling them. It's only a joke and I'd tell them afterwards.

Playing drinking games is good fun. I would persuade my mate to do it with us even if he wasn't keen.

I've been out on the town before and not remembered how I got home. It's ok, I'm always with people who will make sure I'm alright.

My little brother always asks me and my mates for a drink when they come round for a night. It's a pain because he usually throws up, but I let him have it to keep him quiet. It's sometimes quite funny to watch him!

Ask them to discuss, think of arguments on *both* sides, and if possible come to a group consensus. Give each group a piece of flipchart paper and pen so they can scribe their discussions.

Bring the groups together when you feel they have had enough time to come up with some interesting points, and have a small group discussion about each situation, beginning with those who discussed each one, and widening it out to other contributions.

Who is at risk?

Copy onto A4 sheets and laminate the response cards 'At risk' and 'Not at risk'. Using the following drinking habits scenario cards, give each person (or pair, depending on how big the group is) a card and ask them to place them either as at risk or not at risk, according to whether they think their drinking is risky. Use the following principles to decide whether they are at risk:

• Younger people and young children are more at risk from drinking than older adults.
• The recommended safe number of units for an adult male to drink weekly is 21; the recommended safe number of units for an adult female to drink weekly is 14.
• It is recommended that people have at least one alcohol-free day a week.

- Binge drinking (drinking a lot in one session but not necessarily frequently or regularly) is thought to be a very risky way to consume alcohol. Teenagers are more susceptible to alcoholic poisoning than adults, many of whom have their stomachs pumped in casualty, as they have immature livers.
- Alcohol has a cooling effect on the body making being left outside while drunk very risky.
- Alcohol causes dehydration.
- Older people can be more at risk from drinking than younger adults, who have younger livers.
- Most of the date rapes reported have involved spiking drinks with alcohol (not necessarily a 'date rape' drug like rohypnol).

End game

Choose an end game from the selection.

Drinking habits scenario

Jane – aged 17, regularly goes out on Saturday nights with her friends to night clubs. She usually can't remember how she got home.	**Alice** – aged 16, drinks a glass of wine with her parents at mealtimes during the weekends. Does not drink during the week.
Robert – aged 18, goes out on Fridays and Saturdays with his friends to the pub. Regularly drinks 8–10 pints of bitter on nights out, but this could be an underestimate because he usually can't remember how much he has drunk. Never drinks during the week.	**James** – aged 19, works in the construction industry and goes out for a beer every lunchtime. Has two or three beers at the weekend.
Michael – aged 15, hangs around with his mates each night. They usually get through a couple of bottles of vodka two or three times a week as a group.	**Darryl** – aged 12, clubs together with his friends to buy bottles of white cider at the weekends, which they share. They generally spend as much money as they have on it.

Marion – aged 43, drinks a couple of glasses of wine with her evening meal each day.

David – aged 25, works full time, and doesn't usually have time to go out, but two or three times a month will go out with mates to town and get absolutely hammered on strong lager and vodka shots.

Sam – aged 20, at college full time, and also has a part-time job, so doesn't have the time to go out all the time. Sometimes has a beer in the evening with mates, and occasionally goes to town with them where he will drink four or five pints of lager, depending on how much money he has.

Eva – aged 81, has a couple of brandies before she goes to bed to help her sleep each night, because she feels too cold to sleep otherwise.

Ray – aged 8, is given cans of lager by his older brother when his mum is out.

Sophie – aged 13, goes out with her parents on Saturdays to the club where she drinks alcopops all evening.

Trevor – aged 17, drinks lager every day starting when he gets up in the morning. He is unemployed, so he doesn't have anything else to do with his time. He will often end up at friends' houses drinking into the night. Usually they stick to lager because its cheap, but sometimes they drink bottles of whisky between them.	**Brian** – aged 32, drinks a pint of lager every lunchtime with his colleagues from work. He will often go home after work and open a bottle of wine. He always goes to the pub on Saturdays where he drinks lager all evening. Several times he has been involved in a fight outside the pub at closing time.
Denise – 24, is a single mum with an 18-month-old child. She has got in the habit of opening a bottle of wine when she has put him down for the night. She wouldn't admit it, but sometimes she will open a second bottle if she is feeling miserable or tired.	**Michael** – aged 15, doesn't often drink because he usually doesn't have enough money to pool with his friends for a crate. However, on a couple of occasions recently he has got so drunk that he passed out unconscious. His friends took him home but left him on the doorstep as they didn't want to wake his parents.
Michelle – aged 19, drinks every day with her friends, but she feels this is under control because she only ever drinks normal strength lager, and never touches spirits. Last week she found out she was eight weeks pregnant.	**Theresa** – aged 17, only drinks socially, which usually means a couple of pints at the weekend. However, when she is feeling depressed or stressed she always buys a bottle of vodka to drown her sorrows.

Not at risk

At risk

Group session plan: alcohol

Exercise time	Total time	Exercise	Items needed	Facilitator
3 mins	3 mins	Ground rules	Flipchart Pens	
5 mins	8 mins	Opening game		
15 mins	23 mins	What do you know? Distribute all the cards, place the true/not true card in the centre. Each person decides where their card goes. Group discussion.	Alcohol fact or fiction cards, True/not true cards on A4	
3 mins	26 mins	Mix up game		
15 mins	41 mins	Alcohol ethics: small group discussions, the full group discussion	Ethics cards Flipchart paper and pens	
15 mins	56 mins	Who is at risk? Each participant decides whether the person on their card is at risk or not from their drinking. Group discussion	Drinking scenarios At risk/not at risk cards on A4	
4 mins	60 mins	End game		

Drugs

Ground rules discussion.

Opening game: choose an opening game from the selection.

Know about drugs

This exercise builds throughout the session to create a complete picture of each commonly found drug so that young people can be aware, know what they have been offered, and understand the effects and dangers of each.

Begin by making cards of each drug detailed in the slang names exercise. These are then placed so they can have other cards clustered around them as the session develops, but the layout depends on what each individual group situation is like. For example, it may be best to use a wall and have sticky tack on the back of all the cards being used so a wall frieze is created, or there may be a space in the centre of the room that can be used for placing the cards on the floor, around which the participants sit. Each card needs to be big enough for everyone to see clearly from their place in the group. It may make the whole frieze easier to look at if each section is printed on different colour cards (so for example, all the slang names are on yellow card, the effects are on blue, etc.)

Drug slang

Write up the drug slang names shown below so they can be cut up into individual cards. Please note that this list is not exhaustive, and that in some parts of the country there may be regional variations. Some drug slang names are:

Cannabis – marijuana, reefer, weed, skunk, hemp, pot, hash, joint, junk, indica, ganja, Mary Jane, grass, blow, bud, draw.
Heroin – brown, smack, junk, dust, horse, scag, china white.
Cocaine – Charlie, C, snow, toot, rock, coke, rocket fuel.
Amphetamine – speed, crank, billy, copilots, dexies, whizz, flash, phet, uppers, bennies.
Ketamine – Vitamin K, Special K, Ket, K, cat valium.
LSD – acid, tabs, blotters, trips, dots, microdots, Lucy, smilies, purple haze, rainbows.

Ecstasy – love drug, MDMA, echoes, doves, Es, disco biscuits, burgers, Adam, smarties, Mitsubishis.
Rohypnol – forget-me-now, rib, roche, roofies, rope, R-2, mexican valium.
Amyl (or Butyl) Nitrate – poppers, Gold Seal, Liquid Gold, ram, rock hard, TNT, kik, thrust, TNT, locker room.
Magic mushrooms – shrooms, mushies, magics, liberties, buttons.

Share out the cards of slang names among the young people. Each person in turn takes one of their cards and decides what drug it refers to, and places it there. This can then be challenged by others until the correct position is found. If the group is likely to be too critical of those who do not know the answer, or if there are group members who are very unconfident, they can simply present their card to the group who vote on where it should go. The facilitator can then let them know if it is correct.

What does it look like?

On the internet, run an image search to find a good picture of each of the drugs listed above. Print them off, in colour if possible, and laminate. The facilitator then holds up each card in turn with the young people voting on which drug it is. The facilitator then puts each picture with the appropriate drug name as they are guessed.

What class?

Cannabis – class B.
Heroin – class A.
Cocaine – class A.
Amphetamine – class B.
Ketamine – class C.
LSD – class A.
Ecstasy – class A.
Rohypnol – class C.
Amyl (or Butyl) Nitrate – not classified.
Magic mushrooms – class A.

What are the effects?

Put the young people into 10 groups (the size of which will depend on the size of the whole group; it might sometimes be individuals or pairs) and give each group a card with an effect written on (see below). Each group then decides which drug the effect applies to. This is then shared group by group and put in the appropriate place next to the drug name.

Cannabis – makes you feel very hungry.
Heroin – causes drowsiness.
Cocaine – makes your heart beat very fast.
Amphetamine – causes hyperactivity.
Ketamine – gives a feeling of unreality.
LSD – causes hallucinations.
Ecstasy – makes senses more intense.
Rohypnol – causes drowsiness.
Amyl (or Butyl) Nitrate – relaxes muscles.
Magic mushrooms – cause hallucinations.

What are the dangers?

Have a whole group discussion about the dangers of various drugs. Here is some useful information:

Cannabis – no one can overdose on cannabis, but they can become psychologically addicted. It can cause paranoia and mental illness in those with a predisposition towards such conditions, and can also cause sleeping problems. As it can make people feel hungry, it can be linked with weight gain.
Heroin – this can be smoked or injected. It is difficult to overdose if it is being smoked, although there is a risk of fire if people using it become unconscious. Injecting heroin is extremely dangerous (injecting any drug compounds the hazards because it is such a risky activity), and frequently causes death or serious illness because users miscalculate the amount they need and overdose, and it is often unpredictably cut with other substances.
Cocaine – this stimulates the body in a brief but intense way, which includes heart and breathing rate. It can cause heart attacks and fits, and frequent use can damage the inside of the nose. It is easy to overdose on cocaine, especially if it is injected.
Amphetamine – this causes a less intense and longer lasting stimulus to the body, and carries similar risks to the heart. It becomes a class A drug when injected, which increases the general level of risk to health.
Ketamine – can cause mental illness in people with a predisposition towards it. It is extremely dangerous when mixed with alcohol, as it can cause collapse or coma.
LSD – accidents can happen when the user hallucinates, and it can cause anxiety or panic attacks. After a trip, the user can feel exhausted and depressed, and may have flashbacks to the hallucinatory experience.
Ecstasy – this has caused death after just one use in some people, but it is not known why this has happened. Regular use can cause liver or kidney problems, and it is dangerous when mixed with alcohol.
Rohypnol – this is a tranquillizer often used to spike people's drinks so they do not remember what has happened to them. This makes them extremely

vulnerable. Always protect drinks, and do not drink something that has been left unattended.

Amyl (or Butyl) Nitrate – this is sniffed, and can cause skin irritation, and often a headache afterwards. Ingesting it can be fatal, and if spilled on the skin it can cause burns. It is highly flammable, so there is a risk from a combination of smoking and using the product.

Magic mushrooms – some mushrooms that look similar to magic mushrooms are poisonous, and can be fatal. Eating them can cause sickness, diarrhoea and stomach ache. They can cause mental illness in those predisposed towards it.

End game

Choose an end game from the selection.

Group session plan: drugs

Exercise time	Total time	Exercise	Items needed	Facilitator
3 mins	3 mins	Ground rules	Flipchart Pens	
5 mins	8 mins	Opening game		
		Know about drugs	Drug names on cards	
15 mins	23 mins	Drug slang	Slang names on cards	
7 mins	30 mins	What does it look like?	Pictures of drugs	
5 mins	35 mins	What group? Group discussion about the class of each drug, then written next to the name	Pen	
10 mins	45 mins	What are the effects?	Drug effects on cards	
10 mins	55 mins	What are the dangers? Whole group discussion		
5 mins	60 mins	End game		

Bullying

Ground rules discussion

Opening game: choose an opening game from the selection.

Straw poll

Ask the participants to put their hand up if they have been bullied, have known someone who was bullied, or has seen someone bullied (do this as one vote, not three separate ones). Then ask whether they were surprised by the number of people putting their hand up. Ask for some details of some of the circumstances that caused people to put their hand up, but don't push if participants are unwilling. However, it might help some contributions come if the facilitator can cite an instance that falls into one of the three categories.

What is bullying? Through group discussion see if a definition can be reached, and write this down on flipchart paper, which is then displayed in the room.

Where does bullying happen? Facilitate a word shower to see if the participants can identify a range of different places in which bullying occurs. Make sure that this list is as wide as possible, as it could be said to happen wherever there are human beings interacting together in some way. It would appear to be a part of human nature in this respect.

Emotions

In a whole group discussion, make a flipchart list on one half of a piece of paper of all the emotions that someone who is being bullied may feel. On the other half of the paper, make a list of the emotions that someone who bullies people may feel. Compare them briefly to see what the differences are.

Bullying scenario discussion

Divide the whole group into four smaller groups (you may like to use a mix-up game for this). Give each group a copy of Scenario 1. Ask two groups to look at the person being bullied, identifying why they are being bullied, how they think they might feel, what they think they should do to solve it, and what they think the results of this might be. Ask the other two groups to look at the person doing the bullying, identifying why they are doing this, what they are feeling, and what would make them stop.

Join the groups back together after a reasonable length of time to compare what the groups have said and whether they agree or disagree with each other.

Decide on what the plan of action should be for the person being bullied.

Give each group a copy of Scenario 2, and swap round whether they are considering the bully or the bullied. Proceed as for Scenario 1.

End game

Choose an end game from the selection.

Bullying scenario 1

Sarah is 13, and has recently moved into a new area and started to go to a new school. She joined the class mid-year, and was an object of interest for a few days. Her strange accent, and her pristine new uniform causing a few comments among the girls in particular. Sarah was quite shy, so found it very difficult to make new friends, although she tried her best. She found herself being labelled as 'posh', which led on to her being a 'snob', even though she had no idea why this should be. She really missed her old school where she had lots of friends, and very soon she was utterly miserable.

She was particularly in awe of some of the girls in her class, who dressed only just within the letter of the uniform rules, if not the spirit of them, with very short skirts, ties at rakish angles, and boots, rather than boring school clothes. She had managed to make friends with one girl, Marie, but she was very quiet, and didn't seem to join in with the others at break. Sarah kept getting these comments about her being posh, and thinking she was better than the rest of them, which made her very frustrated at the injustice of it all.

One day she was in the school yard with Marie, when a group of girls sidled up to her, with the leader of the short-skirt gang, Beverley, in the front. Beverley walked brazenly up to the pair of them and started making comments about them to the other girls in her gang. When Sarah looked round, Marie had melted away, leaving her on her own. Beverley went right up to her face, pushing her in the chest: 'Come on then, prove you don't think you're better than us. Give us a fight!'

Sarah was now very worried about where this was going, as she was surrounded by a group of very aggressive looking girls all laughing at her. She mumbled something and tried to walk away, but Beverley grabbed her by her tie, and yanked her back: 'Oh no you don't. You have to prove yourself, or we'll never leave you alone. That's a promise.' Just then Sarah heard a teacher come round the corner. She thought he would spot what was going on, but instead he just yelled at some boys on the other side of the field. Beverley hissed in her ear: 'After school, in the park. Be there, or be... scarred for life!' The group then moved off, throwing backward glances towards Sarah, who was now trying to hold back her tears as she gathered up her bag, which had been dropped and trampled in the confusion.

Bullying scenario 2

Mark is 14, and has started going to the local youth club. He's a very good footballer and a tidy pool player, which is partly the reason he joined in the first place. The club has a football team in a local league, which is by far the closest serious team to Mark. He seemed to be ok to begin with, making lots of mates and impressing the football coach with his skills. He had plenty of fans in the club who wanted to be associated with such a good player. He might be famous one day! They queued up to play him at pool so they could say they'd beaten him... although not many of them could!

Things went very wrong one day when Mark was leaving the club. He was walking home through the local park when he suddenly found himself surrounded by a group of boys, some of whom he recognized from the club. Most of them he'd never seen before, and some looked two or three years older than him. Mark was sure he could talk his way out of this, so he kept on walking, wondering if one of them would speak. He didn't have long to wait. The ringleader, Chris, who he'd definitely seen hanging about at the back of the club, but he hadn't had much to do with, stood firmly in his way: 'Where d'you think you're going? You really think you're good don't you!'

At this point he started to push Mark backwards, prodding him in the chest, until Mark came up against one of the other boys in the group, who shoved him hard, saying: 'Watch where you're going will you? Stupid idiot! You did that deliberately didn't you?' Mark went sprawling on the ground at this, but when he tried to pick himself up he found a big boot on his stomach, and a tall leering boy standing over him. He grinned, saying: 'Teach him a lesson, Jack.' Mark then felt a boot in his side, as someone he couldn't even see started to kick him, then made contact with his nose. As blood spurted, Mark saw Chris's face loom in front of his, saying: 'If you know what's good for you, pretty boy, keep away. Don't come to the club, don't come to this park. It belongs to me! Next time you won't even see us coming.'

Group session plan: bullying

Exercise time	Total time	Exercise	Items needed	Facilitator
3 mins	3 mins	Ground rules	Flipchart Pens	
5 mins	8 mins	Opening game		
7 mins	15 mins	Straw poll – Hands up: been bullied, know someone who's been bullied, or seen someone being bullied. Sharing of these experiences.		
5 mins	20 mins	What is bullying? Write a definition of bullying	Flipchart paper and pens	
5 mins	25 mins	Where does bullying happen? Word shower of responses		
5 mins	30 mins	Emotions – what emotions do those who are bullied and those who bully have?	Flipchart paper and pens	
25 mins	55 mins	Bullying scenarios discussion Discuss in four groups the two scenarios (one at a time), with two groups discussing the bully and two the bullied person. Group sharing of small group discussions	Bullying scenarios Flipchart paper and pens for each group	
5 mins	60 mins	End game		

Criminal damage

Ground rules discussion

Opening game: choose an opening game from the selection.

What is criminal damage?

Have a group word shower about what would constitute criminal damage.

A definition of criminal damage is: *Damage caused by someone either deliberately or recklessly to property belonging to someone else.* Examples of criminal damage can include:

- graffiti (using anything like pens, spray paint, carving; it has been known for someone to be prosecuted for writing on the pavement in chalk, although this is not very common)
- scratching cars
- breaking items at home in an argument with a family member
- breaking something in a shop and not paying for it
- breaking a window
- damaging the contents of someone's garden or allotment
- damaging play equipment in a playground
- carving into trees
- disabling speed cameras or CCTV cameras
- egging windows
- throwing missiles at something and damaging it
- writing in library books
- breaking bits off someone's fence
- putting holes in doors or walls in a temper
- pouring corrosive liquid on cars and other items
- throwing snowballs causing scratches or dents
- damaging (or writing on) bus seats (or any other seat like a cinema seat)
- putting cigarette burns in things
- pushing gravestones over
- tampering with telephone network equipment
- damaging parkland
- putting glue in locks
- breaking or obliterating signs

Whether a person committing any of these offences is prosecuted will depend on whether there is someone to press charges, for example, if damage is committed at home, parents have to be prepared to press charges. Some prosecutions will be brought because it is felt to be in the public interest, which applies to public property like park benches, but other charges will be pressed by companies, like railways for damage to stations and associated property.

What are the legal consequences?

It is useful for young people to understand exactly what awaits them should they engage in this kind of behaviour, so the following is a brief description of the current youth justice system as it would work for young people being pursued for criminal damage:

> *Criminal damage is rated by the courts as a 2 on a scale of seriousness that runs from 1 to 8, with 8 being the most serious. This means that acts of criminal damage are likely to be pursued through the courts by police if there is enough evidence to convict. The consequences will depend on what else people have been in trouble for before. Young people will usually follow a pattern of police reprimand, final warning, and then first court appearance resulting in a Referral Order, should they plead guilty in court. If they decide to plead not guilty, the court cannot give a Referral Order, but instead will have to use more serious Youth Rehabilitation Orders. However, it is worth noting that when more serious offences than criminal damage have been committed, this pattern may be circumvented, with matters taken straight to court. Custody is also a possibility at the first court appearance – but not in the case of criminal damage.*

NB: This is the situation currently in England and Wales. The system in Scotland is very different, as young people are required to appear at Hearings rather than in courts. Check the current situation through ringing the local youth offending service, or checking on the internet. Other agencies may also be able to advise.

Who are the victims?

It may seem that criminal damage is not a serious offence and is something that people accept as the norm in our society, but each act has its victims (at this stage, take a moment to ask if anyone can explain what a victim is. Point out that victims can be anyone in some way affected adversely by something that happens, not necessarily just the most obvious person).

Try to imagine a world where there was no graffiti, no park benches with names carved all over them, no broken bottles all over the ground, people could grow plants in their gardens or window boxes without fearing they might be uprooted and strewn about, people not worried that someone might come along and yank their MP3 player headphones from their ears, and public parks had well maintained play equipment for children to play on without fear of damaged items causing injury. It would actually be quite nice to live in a place like that, but it shows how far society has gone from this that we really cannot imagine it!

Ask the participants to discuss in pairs (you might need to use a mix-up game for this) the following criminal damage scenarios on cards (give one set to each pair), deciding who is affected by the action, how they might feel about it (you may like to give groups copies of the emotions cards to refer to; see page 00), and how this might change their future behaviour. You might like to write these up as questions on a board or flipchart, to be referred to during the exercise. Encourage them to think about victims in the widest possible sense, including innocent passers-by, communities as a whole, children who play outside, and animals that may roam the area, both wild and domesticated.

After enough time has been given for each pair to discuss each scenario, ask each pair to bring one of the scenarios to the whole group, giving their answers to the questions asked (ensure that each pair brings a different one – this may influence how many of the cards you give out, but ensure they all have the same selection). Others from the group can add comments to each scenario after the pair have brought their ideas first.

Locally speaking

Focus on the area in which you are situated, and think through the different types of space there are. Encourage a discussion about this in the group, putting the main points raised on the flipchart. For example, there may be council estates, private housing estates, a local park, shopping centre, sports centre, skate park, play area, tennis courts, bowling green or golf course.

With all the different areas identified, either discuss as a whole group the different types of criminal damage that has been noticed there, or split into smaller groups and divide up the areas so each group discusses different areas. Ask them also to discuss who (general people types rather than specific individuals) they think is likely to be responsible for the damage, and why. Then ask them to try to identify some solutions to this as a problem in the area. If possible, come up with a couple of action points that the group could put into practice to improve the area.

End game

Choose an end game from the selection.

Criminal damage scenario cards

An old lady who has lived in the area for 50 years has her daffodils picked and thrown around the street when she is in bed one night	Amy, who is 23 and recently got a new job after being unemployed for a year, finds her car with a scratch all the way down the side of it. It's a new car that she bought with a car loan	One winter Paul finds his motorbike covered in snow that has obviously been thrown as snowballs. When he clears the snow off he finds that the mirrors have been broken
Mary, who bought a park bench in memory of her husband, who died, finds it covered with writing in permanent marker pen	Elaine and her family come home from their holiday to find their windows had eggs throw at them some time ago. It really is dried on now and will take a lot of cleaning	A local cinema owner is shown some seats at the back of his cinema with the cloth is ripped off in several places. He only recently replaced them
A girl returns to her local newsagent some magazines she bought there, as she found they had comments and lewd pictures drawn on in biro throughout	Patrick had an argument with his mum because he didn't want to come off the internet when she told him to, and threw her laptop down the stairs in temper	Mandy comes home from work to find that one of the windows in her living room has a large crack running from top to bottom
Dave goes out in the morning to find the wing mirror on his car has been wrenched off and is lying next to the car	Sally and Debs had an argument, which resulted in Debs grabbing Sally's mobile phone and throwing it into the lake	Fred and Harry (both aged 13) have a competition to see who can hit the light on the train station with a stone, and the light breaks when Fred is successful

Group session plan: criminal damage

Exercise time	Total time	Exercise	Items needed	Facilitator
3 mins	3 mins	Ground rules	Flipchart Pens	
5 mins	8 mins	Opening game		
10 mins	18 mins	What is criminal damage? Word shower about what can be viewed as criminal damage	Flipchart paper and pens	
2 mins	20 mins	What are the legal consequences? Brief overview of the legal system, currently in use in England and Wales		
20 mins	40 mins	Who are the victims? In pairs, then group discussion	Scenario cards, paper and pens, and emotions cards for each pair	
15 mins	55 mins	Locally speaking What types of areas do you have and what are their issues? How can these be improved? Whole group or small group discussion then whole group share	Flipchart paper and pens	
5 mins	60 mins	End game		

Peer pressure

Ground rules discussion

Opening game: choose an opening game from the selection.

Persuasion

Play a game with the participants where they are asked to decide whether they would do a certain action (see the selection below). Those who would do the action are then given an opportunity to persuade those who wouldn't do it with arguments about why it is a good idea. If there are no participants who would be prepared to do the actions, have some ideas so you can do the persuading. (Think in terms of being a dare, if they would make money from it, win a bet, win respect from people, etc.) Take another vote to see whether anyone has changed their mind, and ask them why. This can be done with a few examples. Here are some suggestions.

Would you be prepared to...

Eat an earth worm?
Take a parachute jump?
Walk from John O'Groats to Lands End?
Swim the Channel as part of a team?
Volunteer at a local community project?
Do a 24-hour fast for the Third World, donating the saved money?
Voluntarily give up your mobile phone for a week?
Join a gym and go every week for a year?
Put on a stone in weight?
Go vegetarian?
Give up smoking?
Engage a policeman in friendly conversation?

Discussion

How easy is it to persuade other people to do something you really think is a good idea, even if they don't agree?
What makes someone persuasive?
What makes someone easily persuaded?
What makes you say 'no' to something?

Put the responses on a flipchart, if appropriate.

What is peer pressure?

Ask what the participants think peer pressure is, as this is a phrase that is often mentioned without much explanation.

When they have come up with ideas, either amalgamate their responses into a definition, or assist with this by offering some explanations of the terms. Make sure they know that a peer is someone else their own age group, with whom they might associate. It is not necessarily a friend. Peer pressure is not necessarily a negative concept, as the pressure could be pro-social as well as anti-social.

Scenario discussion

In small groups (use a mix-up game if appropriate), discuss one of the following scenarios, which have been printed and laminated. Give each group paper and pens so they can record their discussion.

Each group presents their scenario and discussed answers to the whole group, with an opportunity for other participants to add their thoughts afterwards.

End game

Choose an end game from the selection.

Group session plan: peer pressure

Exercise time	Total time	Exercise	Items needed	Facilitator
3 mins	3 mins	Ground rules	Flipchart Pens	
5 mins	8 mins	Opening game		
10 mins	18 mins	Persuasion – vote on willingness to try different actions, debate about the advantages, then vote again		
10 mins	28 mins	Discussion questions: How easy is it to persuade someone to do something they don't want to do? What makes someone persuasive? What makes someone easily persuaded? What makes you say 'no' to something?	Flipchart and pens	
7 mins	35 mins	What is peer pressure? Discussion to write a definition of the term.	Flipchart and pens	

20 mins	55 mins	Scenario discussion – in small groups, discuss one scenario in each group, using the questions on the scenario cards as prompts. Each group then brings their scenario to the whole group.	Scenarios Paper and pens for each group	
5 mins	60 mins	End game		

Peer pressure scenario 1

Billy is 12 and has just started at a new school. He met some of his new class-mates in the park the first weekend and, although he felt a bit nervous, rode up to them on his bike. He had never smoked before, but all of them were smoking. They nudged each other and asked him if he wanted to share a ciga-rette. Billy didn't want to make a fool of himself by coughing his guts up, but he also knew that they would laugh at him if he said no.

What should Billy do?

What would you do if you were Billy? Take a vote in your group and see who would agree to smoking and who wouldn't. Write down the reasons.

Billy said yes to the cigarette, and it didn't take him long to get hooked on smoking. He managed to keep it from his mum, who would have gone mad, but it was getting difficult to hide what he was doing, especially since he was spending all his money on cigarettes now.

One day down at the park, Billy's friends lit what he thought was just a roll-up, but it smelled completely different. They told Billy it was a spliff, and asked him if he wanted to try it. Billy had come to rely on the friendship of this group, and wondered whether he would lose it if he said no, or seemed reluctant, but he was also scared by the thought of trying drugs. This was a whole new ball game.

What should Billy do?

What would you do if you were Billy? Take a vote in your group and see who would agree to trying the cannabis and who wouldn't. Write down the reasons.

Billy said no to the spliff, mainly because he felt sure his mum would smell it and then he would be in deep trouble. His friends said that he was a chicken, and went off without him, giving him dirty looks as they went. Billy felt really fed up about this, and now felt like he had no one to hang about with. Worse than that, he lived by the park and knew he would see them every day, which would be really bad if they kept on calling him chicken.

The next day, Billy was riding on his bike through the park when one of them leapt out in front of him. This made him jump and fall off his bike. Picking himself up, he tried to look like it didn't hurt as the rest of the group came out and surrounded him. They pulled out a spliff and said that he would prove himself if he had just one swallow.

What should Billy do?

Billy still said no, so another one of the group said: 'I dare you to. If you don't then you are the biggest chicken around. Who wouldn't have just one swallow?'

What should Billy do?

What do you think Billy actually did?

Peer pressure scenario 2

Jenny is 14, and has been friends with Kelly for years. They both went to high school together and had to sit next to each other because their surnames started with the same letter! This happened in so many lessons that they soon became firm friends. One day, they were shopping in town when Kelly slipped a tube of mascara in her bag, and motioned to Jenny to follow her out of the shop. When they got outside, Jenny asked Kelly what she thought she was doing stealing mascara. Kelly said she didn't have any money, and in any case, the shop was a massive one, so it wouldn't notice losing one item. It wasn't as if anyone was hurt by it. Everyone knows that shops expect to lose a certain amount through shop-lifting, so they make up for it by putting all their prices up.

Next time they went shopping, Kelly said to Jenny: 'I dare you to nick something from this next shop! Not something big, just something they won't notice. It'll give you a real buzz!'

What should Jenny do?

What would you do? Take a vote in your group and see who would agree to shoplifting and who wouldn't. Write down the reasons.

Jenny decided she wouldn't do the shoplifting and tells Kelly. To her surprise, Kelly was really scornful, saying Jenny thought that she was better than Kelly, and this was just her way of showing it. She said all she was asking her to do was nick something that no one would ever notice, so no one would be hurt. She then said that if Jenny was a real friend she would do it because she wouldn't want to make Kelly feel like that.

Jenny felt really confused by this. She knew she didn't want to do any shop-lifting, but she also didn't want her best friend to ditch her for not being supportive.

What should Jenny do? Why?

Jenny still decided that she didn't want to shoplift, so she told Kelly that although she really wanted to stay friends, she wouldn't shoplift to prove it. Kelly was really offhand with Jenny and they didn't go out to town for the next couple of weeks. In fact, Kelly started to hang around with Leanne instead, which really ticked off Jenny, as Leanne could be a real bitch sometimes!

Jenny bumped into Kelly and Leanne in town one day, just as they were coming out of a shop, giggling. Kelly said to Jenny: 'Look what Leanne just nicked! She's really brave – she dares do it even when there are cameras around. I bet you would never dare do that.' Leanne chips in: 'Course she wouldn't, Jenny is a real wimp, and a goody two shoes. You wouldn't catch her doing anything wrong. She's so much better than us!' Jenny opened her mouth to protest, but Kelly interrupted: 'Well maybe you can prove her wrong, Jenny!'

What should Jenny do?

What would you do? Take a vote in your group and see who would agree to shoplifting and who wouldn't. Write down the reasons.

Peer pressure scenario 3

Steve is 16, and has a good group of mates with whom he spends all his time. They tend to hang around the skate park at the weekend, just chilling out. One Saturday they were there as usual when another group came along and started to give dirty looks to Steve and his mates. They didn't usually get any trouble so this was unusual. One of the rivals stepped forwards and started making comments to Steve, who was standing nearest. Some of Steve's friends stepped in and demanded that he take back his words and get out of the park. The other group then started saying they had every right to be there, and that it would be Steve's group who had to leave. One of Steve's mates stepped forward and challenged this, squaring up to the other ring leader. Steve also stepped forward, putting his hand on his mate's shoulder saying: 'Leave it. It's not worth it.' The rival group then turned on Steve, calling him chicken and telling him to get out and leave them to claim the patch.

What should Steve do?

What do you think his friends would think about this decision?

What would you do? Take a vote in your group and see what each group member would do. Write down the reasons.

Steve still kept hold of his temper, because he knew he would end up in trouble with the police if he had a fight with the other group, as he already had a record for fighting. He was determined not to mess up again.

The other group continued to taunt Steve, seeing him as a weak link because he tried to avoid a fight, moving on to calling his family names. One of them started making comments about his kid sister, which really riled him. He turned away, fists clenched, telling himself they weren't worth the hassle. His friends crowded round him, saying in astonishment, 'You're not going to let them get away with that are you?' Steve dug his heels in, and although red in the face, growled that he wasn't going to give them the pleasure. Another comment, about his mum this time, came flying over. Steve's friends started saying: 'Come on Steve, listen what they're saying. You can't let them get away with that... they're disrespecting your family big style!'

What should Steve do now? How can he resist his friends' advice to teach them a lesson for calling his family names?

Steve was at boiling point now, but really didn't want to risk being arrested again. He was worried about the damage he might do if he let rip, feeling the way he did. He shrugged his friends off and angrily walked away, feeling sick.

One of the rivals started joking with one of Steve's gang about him being scared, and not able to stand up for himself. Steve's friend hotly denied this, saying to Steve: 'Come on, prove him wrong. Our whole gang pride depends on you now!'

What should Steve do?

What do you think his friends would think about this decision?

What would you do? Take a vote in your group and see what each group member would do. Write down the reasons.

Peer pressure scenario 4

Alice is 14, and wants to get in with some other girls in her year at school who always seem like they are having more fun than she is! She met one of them after school, who invited her to a party that Saturday night. This was her chance! She immediately said yes, and was already really looking forward to it. She had arranged to meet them beforehand in the park, and when she got there she found they were getting in the mood for the evening with a bottle of vodka. She suddenly felt a little out of her depth. Although Alice had drunk alcohol before, and had been somewhat drunk on a couple of occasions, she realized she might be in trouble if she started drinking this early in the evening. They offered her some of the vodka.
What should Alice do?
What do you think her friends would think about this decision?
What would you do? Take a vote in your group and see what each group member would do. Write down the reasons.
Alice decided she couldn't turn down the drink at this stage, as they might have got fed up with her and left her behind. She was careful to drink a small amount from the bottle, which gave her more confidence that she would be fine... she could handle this ok.

When they arrived she had a can shoved in her hand, and was shown to a dim room with music blaring, full of other young people. There was nowhere obvious to sit, so Alice leant against the wall near where her new friends were chatting up some boys. Alice recognized them as being a couple of years older than them, having left school last year. She held back, until one of her friends introduced her to a few of them, also winking at her while she put some vodka in Alice's can. 'Loosen you up', she said. Alice again had the feeling that control of the evening was not going to be within her grasp, but she thought, well maybe it *will* loosen me up, and took a slug of her drink. She started to feel a bit dizzy as one of the boys asked her who she was and what she enjoyed doing. She started to reply when one of her friends indicated that she was going to fetch them some more drinks from the stash on the floor. Alice had started to feel a bit sick, and couldn't properly concentrate on what the boy was saying.
Should Alice accept another drink?
What do you think her friends would think about this decision?
What would you do? Take a vote in your group and see what each group member would do. Write down the reasons.
Alice decided to accept, and ended up with a plastic cup full of yellowish clear liquid. She had no idea what it was, but drank it anyway. The boy now started to put his arm round her, and suggested they went upstairs. This was totally out of Alice's field of experience and she started to panic. Her friend saw her look and suggested she have the pill she gave her, as it would make her feel 'more friendly'.
What should Alice do?
What would you do? Take a vote in your group and see what each group member would do. Write down the reasons.

Racism

Ground rules discussion.

Opening game

Divide the group into two teams, but ensure that one team (later becoming the Green team) has more members, to bias the game in the Green direction. (Red and Green team sheets follow.) Play a competitive game between the two teams as an opener. A suggestion for this is building a tower with spaghetti (dried!) and marshmallows. Allow a certain amount of time for the building and some time for judging the winner. Encourage competition! If there is any room for doubt make sure the Green team is declared the winner.

Racism experience game

Give each team their team sheet to read, so they can understand something about the character of their team.

Task 1: Choose someone to be interviewed for a job as a public convenience cleaner. The facilitator (who is a Green) interviews both candidates, and shows a blatant bias against the Red applicant, using some of the reasons the Greens hate the Reds to dismiss that candidate. Alternatively, the facilitator can give the job to the Red, telling the Green candidate that they can get a much better job than that, and asking why were they applying for such a lowly position.

Task 2: Choose someone else from each team who is going to join the council for the area. Everyone else currently on the council is a Green. The Greens have to question the Red candidate, and the Reds have to question the Green candidate. Take a vote on who should win (which will probably be the Greens because there are more of them).

Task 3: The teams are now young people in a school yard. They have to decide who they want to be friends with and get into pairs.

Assess the previous tasks, asking to begin with how the Reds felt as they played the game (write the emotion words on a flipchart). Then ask how the Greens felt (add these to the flipchart sheet) being united (if they were!) against the Reds. Did being in a group that felt the same way make them more or less likely to want to get to know the Greens?

How were the friendships at the end made? Were there any cross-colour friendships? What made them make friends across the divide? What made them stick to their own team colour?

Did the Greens as individuals have good reason to dislike the Reds? Did the Reds have any good reason to dislike the Greens?

How do you think this game happens in our society? Who are the Greens and the Reds? What do they feel about each other? Do they have any good reasons for this?

Barriers

What are the barriers between different types of people in our society, and how can they be bridged? Hold a group discussion and, on a flipchart, pair up barriers with some solutions.

End game

Choose an end game that brings the participants together in a supportive way, to counteract the feelings created during the racism game.

Group session plan: racism

Exercise time	Total time	Exercise	Items needed	Facilitator
3 mins	3 mins	Ground rules	Flipchart Pens	
10 mins	13 mins	Opening game – spaghetti and marshmallow towers	Spaghetti and marshmallows. Newspaper to build on. Tape measure	
35 mins	48 mins	Racism game – give each team the explanation of their team's role	Racism game sheet for red and green team	
7 mins	55 mins	Barriers	Flipchart paper and pens	
5 mins	60 mins	End game		

Team sheet

The Greens

You are the Greens. You think you are superior in every way to the other group, who are the Reds. They seem less intelligent than you, cannot work together, and do everything differently from you. You dislike them a lot because the way they do things is really annoying. In fact, you might go as far as to say you hate them! It has been this way ever since they came to live near you. They should never have come, and should have stayed in Redland where they belong, even though they have been here for years now. They speak strangely and eat really revolting food, which smells terrible! This gives them ALL bad breath! You can't understand why they want to be here when they find it so hard to fit in. You are not pleased that they seem to be getting more jobs than the Greens, even if they are jobs you wouldn't particularly want to do.

Team sheet

The Reds

You are the Reds. You think you are superior in every way to the other group, who are the Greens. They seem less intelligent than you, cannot work together, and do everything differently from you. You dislike them a lot because the way they do things is really annoying. The Reds first came to Greenland from Redland years ago, but have found it very difficult to fit in with the locals, who think that the jobs available are beneath them, but you are happy to do them because it's a way of earning an honest living. You can't understand why they get upset because you are doing jobs they aren't prepared to do anyway! You get abuse in the street because you are a Red, and sometimes you give it back to the Greens because you get fed up with it, but this makes you resent them! They are ALL so ignorant! They are always calling you stinky breath, but you feel that they are jealous that their food is all so tasteless.

Part 5

WORKING WITH PARENTS

Parenting

There is much advice available for the parenting of babies and small children, but this seems to peter out when children grow into young people, leaving parents to cope without any further help or advice. The truth is that many parents find adolescence extremely challenging, but do not know where to find help.

Many of the difficulties encountered in adolescence will have begun in earlier childhood, waiting to come out when the going gets tough. Parents who were inconsistent with a toddler, giving in to tantrums because it was easier, have already set the precedent that they can be worn down by difficult behaviour and will not follow through when challenged. Although patterns formed in early childhood are more difficult to change, they are not impossible, but more tenacity is needed on the part of the parent, who has to grow a pretty thick skin fast! This will help them hold out in the face of the demands of, not a toddler this time, but someone possibly taller than them, who can keep an argument going skilfully for days or even weeks! This makes support for parents in these situations extremely important, suggesting that organizations that offer support groups to parents of adolescents with whom they are working, provide a very important service.

The following mixture of discussions and exercises is really designed for individual work with parents, but could be applied to a group. There follows a set of principles that are vital to the successful parenting of adolescents. These can be used with parents in a variety of ways, depending on the relationship built up with the parents concerned and the style of the worker.

Principles for parents

So what is an adolescent?

Adolescence is an interesting age, which is partly a construction of our society. It did not really exist when young people left school at 13 or 14 to go to work to earn a living. They had to grow up quickly, to cope with the responsibility of being a working member of the family, responsible for putting some of the bread on the table. Now young people are largely expected to stay in education or training until they are 18, creating a gap between natural independence and real independence. This gap is adolescence. The advantage of this is that it allows young people to grow up more slowly, learn life skills at leisure, and gain a better education. The disadvantage is that it creates young people who want to be independent, but do not have full autonomy within their lives. It also means some parents continue taking responsibility for tasks their young person should be doing, because there is no rule book on what a young person should be able to do at different ages, like there is in childhood.

When someone has a baby, they have a health visitor telling them what their baby ought to be achieving for themselves – when they should be on solid food, when they should start feeding themselves, when they should be able to make a tower of bricks. There is no one saying to the parents of adolescents when they should be expected to do jobs around the house, when they should be expected to go to bed, or when they should be picking up their own washing from their bedroom floor!

Toddlers will let their parents know when they want to do things for themselves. They will wrestle the spoon out of the parent's hand to feed themselves, and will refuse to get into the pushchair, insisting on walking. Usually this makes life harder for parents to begin with: they have to cope with food all over their child's face, not to mention the floor; it is always slower to let a toddler walk when you could get more things done if they would only get in the pushchair. The trouble with letting the inconvenience stop you is that everyone needs to be able to walk and feed themselves, so those preventing their children learning how to do these things are not helping them. Similarly, parents who do not learn to cope with their adolescent's demands for independence will not help them in a good transition to adulthood.

Obviously the things about which an adolescent wants to be independent differ from those of a toddler, but their methods may be similar. Everyone sees toddlers throwing a tantrum in the street (or more often the supermarket because they cannot have what they want!); very often this is what adolescents do as well. The difference is that it can be far scarier for the parents because their young person is so much bigger, and cannot be tucked under an arm in a removal operation!

Expectations

Go through with the parent (or ask them to do this themselves later) what tasks their adolescent is expected to do for themselves, and then make a separate list of what the parent does for the young person (including tasks that are done for the whole family). Go through the lists together, discussing each point. Ask the parent whether they are surprised by how much they do not expect from their young person! Decide which tasks could be transferred from the parent to the young person – it may be useful at this point to decide what the young person will need to be able to do in order to live independently. Make a plan for when these tasks should be transferred. Stress that this has to be done slowly: any young person suddenly expected to do lots of tasks they previously took for granted will object loudly! The actual transferring of responsibility to the young person from the parents will be done gradually and through negotiation (see later).

Rights and responsibilities

Adolescents will be perfectly happy to have mum clean up after them all the time, but will object to not being allowed out in the evenings, as they will feel that they have a right to a later curfew time. Parents need to point out that rights come with responsibilities, so if the adolescent expects to be treated like a teenager by having a later curfew time, for example, then they need to take on some of the responsibilities of being older and more capable of helping in the home.

Being flexible with the growing need young people have for independence is very hard for parents to cope with, as they instinctively want to protect them and keep them safe. Research has shown that one of the causes of criminal and anti-social behaviour in young people is insufficient parental supervision at a younger age. Therefore, surely, having a tight rein on what young people do is a prime responsibility of parents? The answer to this is yes, but with growing flexibility in what is agreed as they grow up. There will come a time when they need to be able to take full responsibility for their own lives, and if parents have been too prescriptive about this for adolescents, then the adolescents will find it more difficult to put boundaries on their own behaviour: they will be too used to relying on someone else to do it for them. Conversely, if they have had no boundaries set for their behaviour, they will not understand the need for such personal boundaries, and will be equally unable to set them for themselves. Furthermore, they will also not know how to set boundaries for their own children when they have them. Steering a middle course is the only way forward, using negotiation and agreement rather than setting disputed rules in stone.

Family contract

Using a contract can be an effective way of negotiating and agreeing terms of living together, so that everyone is clear about their rights and responsibilities, and is also clear what will happen when they do not comply with what has been agreed. It is most effective if a contract system is up and running before any problems occur, so that dealing with changing demands and challenging behaviour can be part of a process that is already in place. If this has not been done, it can still be effective as a way to bring behaviour back under control, because of the mutual benefits that can be gained by all. It can be a way of negotiating more time using the internet, or later curfew times for older young people, and for the parents a way of transferring responsibility for household tasks to the young person.

Devising a contract needs to happen at a time when everyone has set aside time, no one wants to rush off for a date or to watch TV, and everyone is feeling relatively happy about being there. A good atmosphere can be fostered by providing something nice to eat, and having a family meeting around a table. It could also be followed by a family trip out somewhere mutually enjoyable, to really make the point that it is part of being a well-functioning family. Sometimes parents need to be reminded to spend time with their children when they get older, as young people are just as dependent on their parents' attention and good favour as young children, but are less likely to show it (or may show it obliquely with poor behaviour!)

The contract needs to consist of what everyone is prepared to do around the home (it would be more effective if it covered every member of the family, not just a 'problem teen'), with maybe a pool of jobs that need to be allocated at a later date. This needs to move the young person on from their starting position, but not overburden them immediately so that they lose faith in the process being mutually beneficial. There also needs to be a section on expected behaviour in the house, which can include parents, who also need to stick to agreed ideas, such as only smoking outside the house, or only eating downstairs (try to phrase them positively, rather than end up with a list of 'do nots'). Then there needs to be a section of expectations for each individual, which can be written next to their expected jobs. This is where the bedtimes, curfew times, internet allowances, etc are agreed. Discuss the young person's idea, then the parents', then there needs to be a compromise between the two. The individual behaviour section should also include what the parents do, as the young person might want their mum to knock before going in their room, for example. Parents will have reasons for their opinions, like wanting their young person home by a certain time, and they need to communicate these properly, rather than just insisting. It would be unwise to refuse any negotiation at all, as the process is more likely to be successful if the young person feels they have gained something, which might be an extra half an hour with their friends. If a young person won't agree to anything reasonable, then the process should be delayed for a week before reconvening the meeting, but leaving all family members with a clear idea of the benefits for all of an agreed contract.

All of the agreements need to be written up and preferably signed by all members of the family. There needs to be a date set to review the contract to see how it is going, and whether any changes need to be made. There then needs to be a date set for a complete re-discussion of the contents of the contract, so that bedtimes, etc can be renegotiated if necessary (this could be in six months time). That way, the young person knows the arrangement, while currently set in writing, will be reasonably reviewed as they change and grow older.

Sanctions and rewards

What happens if the contract is not being adhered to? They are consistently coming in 20 minutes late for example, which parents feel is making the agreement pointless. Part of the discussions on agreed behaviours need to include what will happen when they do not comply with what they have agreed (which is why it is so important that they agreed in the first place!) This could happen before the main contract is written or immediately after, but it definitely needs to be in place straight away, or there will be a situation where the parents do not know how to react to an infringement, choose a sanction that makes the young person feel resentful, and thereby lose their agreement to the rest of the contract.

Sanctions depend very much on the individual and what they would view as being a punishment. It should not be so severe that parents end up reluctant to use it, or something that is so inconvenient that they use that as a reason not to bother. The punishment needs to be immediate, short term, and viable. Sanctions will also depend on the age of the child or young person, so there might be a range of sanctions for different members of the family.

Do not put in sanctions for parents if they do not keep to their side of the contract, as they need to give the message clearly that they are in charge, not the young person, but the young person does need to know they have a right to point out to the parent if they have not kept to the agreement: parents then need to accept responsibility if the system is to be successful.

Suggestions include no internet for one day, being grounded for a day, no TV for the evening, no access to their games console for a day, some loss of pocket money, having to come in earlier the following night, not being allowed a certain item or service (see above) until a certain job is completed. Notice that no sanction is so severe that it will affect the whole family for weeks, or so inconveniencing that the parents won't be able to follow through. They are very short lived, allowing for a new day the next day (or the day after that!) Parents need to make absolutely sure when a sanction is used that the young person knows exactly why it is being used, and how long it will be in effect for, and that they can point to it on the agreed sanctions list. For example: 'Simon, you were late in tonight. It's now 10:45 and you agreed to be in by 10 pm; because of that you're not allowed to go out tomorrow night.'

Rewards are equally important, and should be discussed at the same time as sanctions. Young people like to be rewarded, but this has to be in the right way for them. They have to see the reward as a reward, or it will not be an incentive for good behaviour! There needs to be a discussion between parents and young people about what the young people would view as a reward, and what the parents are prepared to do. There has to be a balance here, so rewards reflect the value of what has been done. It is important, therefore, that parents do not promise the world to their young person, and find that they soon cannot afford to carry out their promise. Suggestions could include making receipt of pocket money contingent on completion of their jobs (as specified in the contract), giving them their favourite magazine for a good week on the contract, extra internet time above the agreed amount (but not if this is too contentious an issue), extra TV time, a parent and young person trip on Saturday to a local fast food place. Care needs to be taken about making whole family trips contingent on behaviour, as this could create sibling issues if one person's behaviour always cancels a trip out. However, a whole family trip out could happen after a review of the contract, if it has been going well, or just as an unexpected treat from a parent who feels things are more under control.

At the end of this section there is an example of a reward chart, which is a visual way of recording how well a child or young person is doing in reaching their goal. It is important to have small steps towards a goal that is not too distant. It is also important not to make the reward contingent on success every day, which is why there are no days identified on the chart. Identifying days implies that there has to be uninterrupted success, which may not be realistic and is setting them up the fail. If they have to gain stickers/ticks every day to get a reward on the Saturday, what incentive is there to behave well for the rest of the week if they fail on Monday?

Some words of warning about using rewards: timing is very important. If the young person gets the reward *before* doing the required behaviour, they are much less likely to actually do it. If they persist in wanting the agreed reward in advance, the parent must be strong in not giving in ('*When* you have… *then*…').

Be wary about the way in which a reward is promised, so it doesn't end up as bribery for something they really should be doing anyway. For example, there have been parents who have promised their young person £5 for going to school, if they are refusing. This can be tempting, especially if the problem is acute, but the message here is, 'You don't have to go to school unless I pay you.' Pocket money could be contingent on going to school, as it can be taken away, as well as given, but assumes that normality is school attendance (even if it isn't at the moment). The other problem with giving a child £5 for going to school is that it is unsustainable – parents are unlikely to be able to keep it up, giving the young person a feeling of injustice if they go to school and the parent cannot afford this 'agreed' reward, the result of which would be no more school attendance… until the parent can pay again!

Praise

Much is said about praising young children, but adolescents need praise just as much. They may not respond in the same way as a young child, but are likely to store positive comments for private appreciation later! Many parents say that there is nothing to reward in their young person's behaviour. It's tempting to think like this when things seem awful, but it's very unlikely to be true. If a young person is behaving horrendously for 50 per cent of the time, then 50 per cent of the time they are not behaving as badly. They may not be brilliant in the other 50 per cent, but they are not actually causing any grief. This is when the parents need to do an incredibly difficult thing and put aside the hurt, anguish and anger they feel about the appalling behaviour, and try to spot when they are being ok. Catch them when they are being ok, and give them some positive feedback or praise. For example, the young person might come in, sit on the sofa and watch TV. What's to praise about that? If praise is to be effective as a behaviour modifier, then it needs to be used whenever possible, so the parent could come in, sit down also, watch some of the programme, and comment about how much they enjoy their young person's company… and SMILE at them! This can happen in about five minutes, so it doesn't require the young person to be quiet for too long! The young person will like the positive feedback, even if they don't seem as if they do, and are then likely to find other ways of getting it, *if* the parent is able to keep on spotting when they are not behaving badly. Positive behaviour is more likely if this is pursued.

Parents need to be very careful not to give with one hand and take back with the other. For example, by saying: 'I enjoy spending time with you – it's a shame you're not always this nice' the parent has, in one stroke, reminded the young person what is actually expected of them, which is poor behaviour. Therefore this is more likely to be what follows!

An exercise to do with parents is to get them to record on a diary sheet (see the end of this section) when they have given praise to their young people, and why. This not only focuses attention on what the young person is doing right, but also focuses the parent's attention on how much they are giving positive feedback to their young people. Actually making a note of this will encourage an increase in praise, and should change the situation in a positive way. (If the balance of praise to admonishment seems too skewed towards the latter, then it would be worthwhile for the parent keeping two diary sheets for a week – one recording praise and one recording admonishment, so the balance can be discussed.)

Attitudes

Attitudes are catching! If someone feels 'got at' then they will be defensive back. Parents have an opportunity to mould the atmosphere in their home by their attitudes. If a young person comes home from school to be greeted with a list of the things they haven't done, or worse, if they are ignored, then they are unlikely to feel positive, and less likely to behave well as a result. There may be good reason for a parent to feel frustrated or annoyed with their young person, but if they greet them with it, they are unlikely to end up with a positive outcome. It is always best to confront behaviour issues in a controlled and timely way.

Similarly, getting up in the morning can be very difficult, and can cause problems within households, but there will be less stress and friction if parents have decided to have a positive attitude at the outset. Therefore, it can be a good exercise to use the diary sheet again but this time to record how they have greeted their young person when they have met up after some time apart (first thing in the morning, after school or after work, when they come in for the night, etc) and what the response was. This is difficult if one of the behavioural issues is linked to these times, but can also show the value of positive attitudes and praise if, when things go well, the young person gets a positive reception. In addition, this is teaching them important social skills that allow them to get on with others who will be a part of their life.

Consistency

This word has to be one of the most important – young people can spot inconsistency whenever it occurs and they can use it for their own benefit, but most often they feel the unfairness of it. This then perpetuates poor behaviour.

When the thwarted toddler throws himself on the floor in a screaming tantrum in the supermarket because his mum won't buy him a toy, what does he learn if she relents and gets him the toy anyway? He learns that if he really pushes, his mum will give in. Therefore, if she holds out a bit longer next time, it just takes a longer, louder tantrum to get what he wants. The mum unfortunately has created a situation in which she cannot win, because she knows he will always beat her in the end, so it's easier just to give in. Teenagers may well already have learnt this lesson as toddlers (ask parents to think back and try to remember how they dealt with their terrible 2-year old), but in any case, will give it another go now. They know which buttons to press to really make their parents want to give in, and if there are two parents, they will know who will give in first, and concentrate on them. Yet, what does the teenager learn from finding that aggression gets them what they want? They learn to deal with their problems through aggression. Often, this will also be seen in other settings, like school, which shows the value of clear agreed boundaries, which are rigorously applied when challenged in an inappropriate way at home.

Dealing with a tantrum in teenagers is largely the same as with toddlers, by directing attention away from the attention-seeking behaviour and onto something else. There is another aspect to consider however, as teenagers are so much bigger than toddlers – the tantrum has to be safe to ignore. If it is not, because the parent or someone else (or the young person themselves) are in danger, then alternative help should be sought, possibly through the police. The advantage of a teenager having a tantrum is that it is usually safe to walk out and leave them to it, which would not be possible with a toddler.

There are some important guidelines for parents to consider:

- If you have agreed to do something, make sure you do it. This includes punishments that have been threatened, rewards that have been promised, and actions that have been agreed.
- If certain behaviours have been agreed as being unacceptable, follow through with an agreed sanction if they occur.
- If there are two adults acting in a parenting capacity within the household, make sure you agree how issues will be tackled, and stick to it. Communicate with each other so you cannot be divided and conquered!
- Do not allow yourself to be ground down by tantrums, aggression, or unacceptable behaviour – deal with these in the agreed way with the agreed sanctions.
- Think carefully before you say 'no' to something. Do you really mean it, or will you think about it later and change your mind? This implies to young people that they can change your mind, encouraging them to nag until you do. Only say 'no' when you really mean no!
- Say 'yes' to some things! If all they ever hear is 'no', young people will cease to ask and just take it upon themselves to do it anyway, or else just feel more and more resentful.
- Build quality time with your young person into your lives. It may seem as if they don't want to spend any time with you, but you'll be surprised at what they might enjoy!
- Take *every opportunity* to praise your young person, and make sure this is pure praise and not an opportunity to have a dig at them for not always being like that!
- Never promise a reward it is not practical to keep on delivering, or a punishment that is so harsh that the next logical step is to chop off their head!

(With thanks to Jonny Cohen for many 'parenting' conversations, and for honing my skills through the running of many parenting groups!)

Diary Sheet

Day/date	When?	What for?
Monday		
Tuesday		
Wednesday		
Thursday		
Friday		
Saturday		
Sunday		
Total		

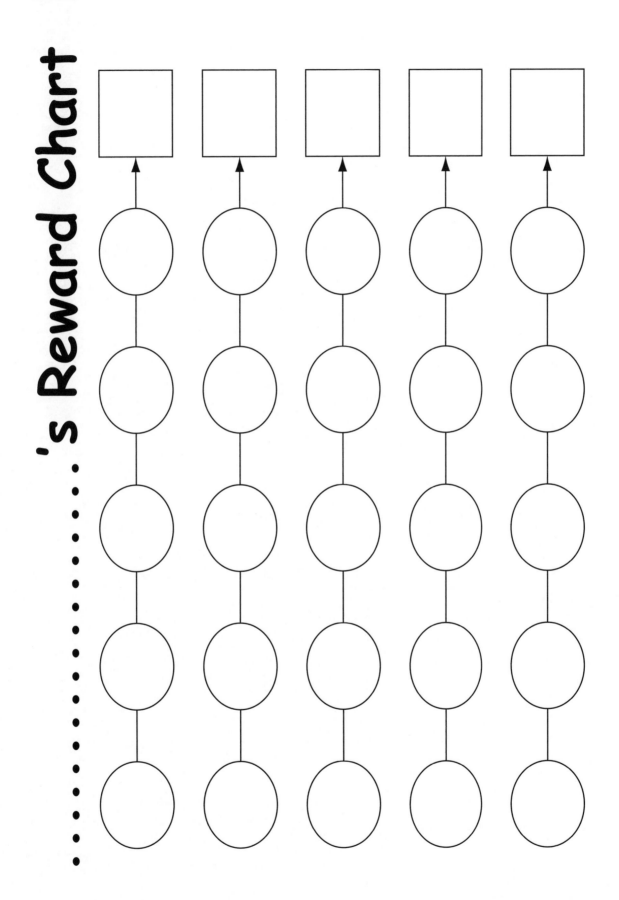

Bibliography

Beinhart, S, Anderson, B, Lee, S and Utting, D (2005) *Youth at Risk? A national survey of risk factors, protective factors, and problem behaviour among young people in England, Scotland and Wales*, London, Communities That Care

Farrington, D P (1997) *Human Development and Criminal Career*, in Maguire, M, Morgan, R and Reiner, R, *The Oxford Handbook of Criminology*, 2nd edn, Oxford, Oxford University Press

Gardner, H (1999) *Intelligence Reframed: Multiple intelligences for the 21st century*, New York, Basic Books

Graham, J and Bowling, B (1995) *Young People and Crime*, Home Office Research Study 145, London, Home Office

Honey, P and Mumford, A (1982) *The Manual of Learning Styles*, Maidenhead, Peter Honey Publications

Honey, P and Mumford, A (2006) *The Learning Styles Questionnaire, 80-item version*, Maidenhead, Peter Honey Publications

Kolb, D (1984) *Experiential Learning: Experience as the source of learning and development*, Englewood Cliffs, NJ, Prentice-Hall

McGuire, J (1995) *What Works? Reducing offending*, Chichester, John Wiley & Sons

Moran, P, Ghate, D and van der Merwe, A (2004) *What Works in Parenting Support? A review of the international evidence*, DfES Research Report RR574, Norwich, HMSO

Rutter, M, Giller, H and Hagell, A (1998) *Antisocial Behaviour by Young People*, Cambridge, Cambridge University Press

Salter, K and Twidle, R (2005) *The Learning Mentor's Source and Resource Book*, London, Sage

Salter Hampson, K (2008) *Setting up and Running a Peer Listening Scheme*, London, Routledge

West, D and Farrington D P (1973) *Who Becomes Delinquent?*, Oxford, Heinemann

Youth Justice Board (YJB) (2005) *Risk and Protective Factors*, London, Youth Justice Board for England and Wales

www.cjscotland.org.uk

www.vark-learn.com

www.yjb.gov.uk